A CHART HISTORY

OF

THE CIVIL WAR

1861 - 1865,

WITH NUMEROUS SHADED MAPS

SHOWING THE PROGRESS OF THE

UNION ARMIES

IN DIFFERENT CAMPAIGNS AND DURING DIFFERENT
YEARS.

FOR THE USE OF SCHOOLS.

———

By J. W. GIBSON.

CHICAGO,
A. FLANAGAN, PUBLISHER.

MAPS AND MAP EXERCISES.

		Page
I.	Territorial Growth of the United States,	16-17
II.	Field of Operations in the West,	30-31
III.	Confederate Line of Defense in the West, Jan. 1, 1862	34-35
IV.	Confederate Line of Defense in the West, April 1, 1862,	40-41
V.	Confederate Line of Defense in the West, close of 1862.	44-45
VI.	The Seat of War in the East,	50-51
VII.	The Peninsular Campaign,	54-55
VIII.	Showing Lee's First Invasion of the North,	56
IX.	Virginia—Confederate Line of Defense—'62 and '63,	59
X.	Grant's Vicksburg Campaign,	64-65
XI.	Chattanooga and Vicinity,	70-71
XII.	Territory Occupied by Confederates at Close of 1863, West,	74-75
XIII.	Virginia and Vicinity—Lee's Second Invasion.	78-79
XIV.	Atlanta Campaign—Georgia,	87
XV.	Of the West—Sherman's March Through Georgia,	92-93
XVI.	Virginia—Grant's Overland Campaign,	100-101
XVII.	Virginia at Close of 1864,	104-105
XVIII.	Sherman's Movements from May 1, 1864, to May 1, 1865,	110-111

CONTENTS.

CHAPTER I.

Direct Causes—Slavery—Fort Sumter—Indirect Causes—Reasons for Differences Between the People of the North and the South—Beginnings of Slavery in America—About the Constitution—Conditions Favorable to Slave Labor—Missouri Compromise—Mexican War—Republican Party—Dred Scott Decision—Kansas Troubles—Sumner Outrage,   -   9-20

CHAPTER II.

How the Army was Organized—Needs of an Army—Difficulties in Supplying an Army—Home Life of a Soldier—Preparations for War—Why the South was Better Prepared—Strength of the North—Hopes of the South,   -   -   -   -   -   -   -   -   -   -   -   -   21-25

CHAPTER III.

Military Events of 1861—Baltimore—Western Virginia—Bull Run—Missouri —Along the Coast—Kentucky—Trent Affair—Summary of 1861,   -   26-31

CHAPTER IV.

1862 in the West—The Objectives—Commanders and Positions—Mills Spring —Fort Henry—Fort Donelson—Island No. 10—Pittsburg Landing— Siege of Corinth—Farragut's Operations at Mouth of Mississippi— Perryville—Iuka and Corinth—Stone River—Review of 1862 in the West,   -   -   -   -   -   -   -   -   -   -   -   -   33-47

CHAPTER V.

In the East, 1862—Study of Virginia—Shenandoah Valley—Routes to Richmond—Merrimac and Monitor—Peninsular Campaign—Lee's First Invasion of the North—Fredericksburg—Synopsis, 1862, in the East, - 48-61

CHAPTER VI.

Congress—Conscription Act—Emancipation Proclamation—War in the West, 1863—Vicksburg—Chattanooga and Chickamauga—Battle of Chattanooga—Synopsis in the West, 1863—Armies and Commanders in the West,   -   -   -   -   -   -   -   -   -   -   -   -   62–75

CHAPTER VII.

Events in the East, 1863—Chancellorsville—Lee's Second Invasion of the North—Gettysburg—Synopsis of 1863—General Results,   -   -   77–81

CHAPTER VIII.

Changes in the Army—Conditions at Beginning of 1864—Atlanta Campaign—Farragut at Mobile Bay—Hood's Movement Northward—Sherman's March to the Sea—Franklin and Nashville—Synopsis in the West, 1864,   -   -   -   -   -   -   -   -   -   -   82–95

CHAPTER IX.

War in the East, 1864—Wilderness—Spottsylvania—Bloody Angle—Soldiers Suffering—Cold Harbor—Grant South of the James—Sheridan in Shenandoah Valley—Synopsis in the East, 1864—General Results, 1864,   -   -   -   -   -   -   -   -   -   96–105

CHAPTER X.

Closing Events, 1865—Pontoons—Sherman Moves North from Savannah—Wilson's Raid—Army of the Potomac—Commanders and Battles—Confederate Armies and Commanders—Confederate Armies Surrendered—The Close—Sheridan in the Valley—Battle Scene—Five Forks—Lee Surrenders—Conclusion,   -   -   -   -   -   -   107–117

INTRODUCTION.

The general movement throughout the nation to have the American flag float over every school-house is an indication of a feeling in the minds of thoughtful people that there is a need of some method by which the minds of the youth may be drawn to realize the value of an American citizenship. In other words, there is a need calling for the teaching of patriotism.

The flag is but a symbol. The manhood of America should have an intelligent idea of what it symbolizes. Man may know and appreciate the liberties he enjoys, but he should also know the cost of those blessings.

An intelligent study of the history of the nation is the only sure way of inculcating a love of country, and an appreciation of its value. The author of this little book, from many years' teaching, knows from painful experience the woful lack of information, among even graduates of our high schools, concerning the great events of 1861–1865.

The events of that period were so stupendous that our school histories can afford the space but to touch the most important occurrences. Events that cost the death and suffering of thousands of men are told in a single sentence.

There is not sufficient ground-work given to lead to fuller reading and investigation of the subject. It is hoped by this book to give sufficient outline to lead to greater interest, and therefore to further reading.

What was done, why (and results), where, when, and who did it, are the five prismatic colors that make the white light of history.

In this book emphasis is placed on the first three. A knowledge of the *why* and the *where* in the mind of the student is essential to clear historic vision.

CHAPTER I.

CAUSES OF THE GREAT CIVIL WAR IN AMERICA.

Direct Causes.—Slavery was the *direct* cause of the civil war in the United States. By the middle of the 19th century, public opinion in all the more civilized communities, outside of our own, had become strongly opposed to the idea of human slavery.

Serfdom existed in Russia until 1863. Slavery in Brazil is in process of extinction, while the Spanish colonies still continue to hold men in bondage. In 1860 our own "Land of the Free" held more slaves than could be found in all other civilized countries combined. When in 1860 the Republican party came into power by the election of Abraham Lincoln as President, the more Southern states became alarmed for the safety of the institution of slavery. Mr. Lincoln and the Republican party did not claim to have any power or right to interfere with slavery in the states where it already existed, but proposed to keep it out of the territories.

The South reasoned correctly when it said that the final result of keeping slavery out of the territories, would be the overthrow of the institution. Immediately the Gulf and South Atlantic States began to plan for secession, and South Carolina, taking the lead, seceded December 20, 1860. The example of South Carolina was soon followed by Mississippi, Florida, Alabama, Georgia, Louisiana and Texas. In February, 1861, delegates from the seceding states met at Montgomery, Alabama, and formed a new government under the name of The Confederate States of America. Jefferson Davis, of Mississippi, was chosen President, and Alexander H. Stephens, of Georgia, Vice-President.

These states at once took measures to get possession of the forts, arsenals and other property of the United States within their borders.

General Twiggs, who commanded in Texas, surrendered all the U. S. forces under him to the Confederate States.

Fort Sumter.—Not all the important posts along the coast were surrendered, among them Fort Sumter, controlling the harbor of Charleston, South Carolina. Major Robert Anderson, of Kentucky, commanded at this place, and great interest centered in the operations around Charleston.

South Carolina demanded the surrender of Fort Sumter. President Buchanan refused. It must be remembered that these events took place before Mr. Lincoln was inaugurated, which inauguration transpired March 4, 1861.

The firing on Fort Sumter and the American flag by the Confederates under General Beauregard, on the morning of April 12, 1861, resounded like an electric shock throughout the North and South, to the extremes of East and West. The boom of the cannon at Fort Sumter startled the North from its dazed condition, and it realized for the first time that war was in the land. All sections were aroused to immediate action. In quick succession all the other slave-holding states, except Delaware, Maryland, Kentucky and Missouri, joined the Confederacy. These states, with West Virginia, remained loyal to the Union, though many individuals within their borders joined the Confederate army. Many good men up to this time had fears that patriotism in America was a thing of the past, but when occasion called for patriots, they came in ready response. Eighty thousand from the free states alone answered Mr. Lincoln's call for 75,000. Thus commenced the civil war, a war of desperate fighting and terrible suffering. A most intense feeling of hatred existed between the two sections. In ordinary war between two nations, contention ceases and peace follows, when one nation finds that it is unable to successfully resist the other; but in the civil war it was a life and death struggle. Were the South successful in leaving the Union, other sections would claim the same right to secede. As a result, a few decades would find what is now a proud nation, separated into numerous, independent states. Europe and South America would thus be repeated. Commercial strife and standing armies jealously watching each other would be the result. The question with the North was, shall we fight it out now and settle the strife for all time, or shall we leave it for future generations to determine? If the nation survived, the Confederacy must die; if the Confederacy lived, the nation would die. The Confederacy died, and with it slavery for which it fought.

REMOTE CAUSES OF THE REBELLION.

Some Reasons for the Differences Between the People of the North and the South.—In order to understand clearly the true causes which led to this unhappy strife between these two sections, speaking the same language, and living under the same laws, it is necessary to go back in history to study the conditions which have tended to separate them. Though the Southern people in their support of slavery placed themselves behind other parts of the civilized world, it must not be assumed that they were wanting in those attributes of character which go to make up a broad and generous manhood and civilization. They were entangled in a social system that had grown up among them, and had its roots reaching far back into their history. The people who settled these two sections, the North and the South, though both of English origin, were quite different.

The character of the settlers of the seventeenth century stamped itself on the generations following. During much of this century there was great religious and political strife in England. Most of the settlers of the North came to America because of religious oppression in the mother country.

In former times it was considered disloyal to one's king and country not to conform to the state religion. Multitudes in different ages have had their fidelity to religious convictions tested, even to the martyr's death. Some of the time it was the Puritan who suffered, sometimes the Quaker, and at others, the Roman Catholic who endured persecution for the cause he believed to be right. The Puritans of England sought a purer system of faith and worship, in opposition to all religious forms. The Cavaliers were loyal to both the state religion and their king.

The Puritans were largely from the middle classes—the yeomanry, the pride and support of England. The Cavaliers belonged largely to the aristocracy and nobility.

The representatives of these two elements of society in coming to America settled in different parts of the country, and were separated from the beginning by these characteristics and religious differences. New England was settled by the Puritans, Pennsylvania by the Quakers, Maryland by the Roman Catholics, who all sought an asylum from religious oppression.

Virginia and much of the South was settled after the first twenty years, largely by the other class for financial and commercial reasons. The northern section from the nature of the climate and soil combined, together with the sturdy character of the people, was occupied by small farmers and manufacturers.

The people of the South brought with them from England the idea of large estates, and the climate and soil aided to perpetuate this ideal. The one section became a manufacturing community in which cities and schools multiplied. The other became agricultural with few cities, and fewer educational advantages except to the wealthy.

The Beginning of Slavery in America.—In 1619 a Dutch trading vessel brought some negroes to Jamestown, whom they sold to the settlers for slaves. Thus but twelve years after the first settlement, slavery was planted in America. Here was sown the germ of discord which brought forth bitter fruit. It is interesting to note that near Jamestown, the seed-bed of slavery, was fought some of the most desperate battles in its support, that but a few miles distant are Richmond, Petersburg and Appomattox, all associated with its final overthrow.

In contrast it is well to note that in the North, Harvard college was founded but seventeen years after the settlement at Plymouth; plantings of two very different institutions—slavery and schools. Each bore its corresponding harvest. Slavery spread through most of the colonies, but slave labor was unprofitable in the North, and gradually died out.

Northwest Territory.—By the famous ordinance of 1787 organizing the Northwest Territory, slavery was prohibited within its boundaries. Washington and Jefferson, though both slave-holders, wished to exclude slavery from all territory not organized into states. This shows the anti-slavery sentiment even at this early date.

About the Constitution.—A few years' test was sufficient to prove the " Articles of Confederation," which had been adopted formally in 1781, a failure. The present Constitution was framed, and, after a long struggle, was adopted, and became the supreme law of the land, in 1789. The Constitution is a compromise between two conflicting principles of government ; one holding to the idea of a strong central government, with little power left to the states, the other favored giving most of the power to individual states, leaving only a limited, delegated power to the general government. Neither extreme was satisfied with the Constitution as adopted. Neither was probably right, as it has proven a most happy compromise on the balance of power between the overshadowing, dangerous centralization of power on one hand, and the discord and weakness arising from too much authority in the hands of individual states, on the other. Since the adoption of the Constitution there have been two classes, one favoring a strong central government, the other advocating state rights. The idea that a state could nullify a United States' law, or leave the Union if it so desired, was not confined to the South. But it became a more fixed doctrine in that section through the teachings of John C. Calhoun, of South Carolina. This state attempted in 1832 to nullify the United States' law in regard to tariff. This doctrine of secession might have remained through all time a mere theory of government, had not the overshadowing question of slavery brought it into prominence. But the Constitution compromised also on the subject of slavery. This was not so fortunate as the other compromise, though probably necessary in order to establish the present government. The Constitution could not have been adopted had not concessions been made by both parties.

As an indication of the sensitiveness on the subject of slavery at the time of the adoption of the Constitution, the word *slave* does not appear in it until used in the XIIIth amendment, which abolishes slavery in the United States. "Persons held to service or labor" is the term used.

The framers of the Constitution hoped and expected that slavery as an institution would die a natural death.

Conditions Favorable to Slave Labor.—The climate, soil, and products of the South made large estates and slave labor more profitable than in other parts of the country. The invention of the cotton gin by Eli Whitney, in 1793, was another aid in the same line. Before this invention it was a slow, tedious process to separate the seed from the cotton wool, and slave labor, as a result of this invention, became more than ever valuable.

From this time until the close of the civil war, the question of the extension of slavery in the Union became a subject of strife. The struggles occurred whenever a new state was to be admitted to the Union, or a new territory added to its dominion. Each section sought to obtain the balance of power. As the free states claimed no right to interfere with slavery already existing in a state, the conflict was necessarily over the admission of new states and the growth of territory.

The Missouri Compromise.—At the close of the Revolutionary war, the Mississippi River was the western boundary of the United States, but Spain held the mouth of this river. Slavery had been excluded from the North West Territory, but permitted south of the Ohio River. In 1800, Spain ceded that vast territory lying directly west of the Mississippi River, known as Louisiana, to France.

In 1803 the United States bought this territory of France for $15,000,000. In 1812 Louisiana, a part of this purchase, lying at the mouth of the river, entered the Union as a slave state. When in 1819 Missouri applied for admission into the Union as a slave state, the anti-slavery people objected. The difficulty was settled by the "Missouri Compromise." By this bill Missouri was admitted as a slave state, but slavery was to be forever excluded from the territory north of 36°—30', the southern line of Missouri. A glance at the map will show that at that time most of the territory was north of this line. This appeared to be much in favor of the North. But more territory was to be added to the constantly increasing possessions of the nation, causing great disturbance to its peace.

Mexican War.—In 1845 Texas, having previously gained its independence of Mexico, applied for admission to the Union. The North opposed this for two reasons : it would result in war with Mexico and add more slave states to the Union. Texas was admitted, and in consequence came the Mexican war. As a result of this war, the United States acquired all that large territory west of the Rocky Mountains and south of Oregon. By a treaty with England in 1846, the disputed tract of Oregon and Washington became a part of the United States. When in 1850 California applied for admission as a free state, the old slavery question again appeared.

As a compromise different bills were passed covering the following propositions :

   1. California was admitted as a free state.

   2. Utah and New Mexico were organized as territories with the privilege of admission as free or slave states as each might choose.

   3. Texas boundary line was established.

   4. The "Fugitive Slave Law" was passed.

   5. An act providing for the suppression of slave trade in the District of Columbia was passed. The Fugitive Slave Law aroused much bitterness of feeling in the North. This agitation showed its determination in large conventions of the indignant people of the North, and in the aid given to slaves escaping from bondage. From this time the bitterness of feeling between the North and the South grew in intensity. In 1854 Senator Stephen A. Douglas, of Illinois, introduced a bill to organize Kansas and Nebraska into territories, and to permit the slave-holder to take his slaves there. This bill became a law, thus practically repealing the "Missouri Compromise," as some of these territories lay north of 36°—30′.

EXERCISE ON MAP I.

TERRITORIAL GROWTH.

Name the thirteen original states.

There are now sixteen occupying the same territory.

Name the other three.

Why and when was each separated from the original state?

What was the western boundary of the United States at the cl
of the Revolution?

What states were carved out of the North West territory?

What state claimed Kentucky, and why? Tennessee, and wh
Mississippi, and why? Alabama, and why?

Why did Virginia, Connecticut and Massachusetts claim a par
the North West territory?

(A suggestion: Trace the north and the south boundaries
each of these states, to see where they strike the North W
territory.)

Give account of the Louisiana purchase.

How many states have been formed from the Louisiana purcha

Are there any territories yet remaining in this purchase?

From whom, and when was Florida purchased?

How and when did Texas become a part of the Union?

How and when did the Oregon country become a part of
Union?

What was the result of the annexation of Texas?

What states and territories are included in the territory obtai
from Mexico as a result of the Mexican war?

Trace the Missouri Compromise line.

What was the real "Mason and Dixon's line"?

Why was the boundary between the free and the slave st
afterward called the Mason and Dixon's line?

MAP I.

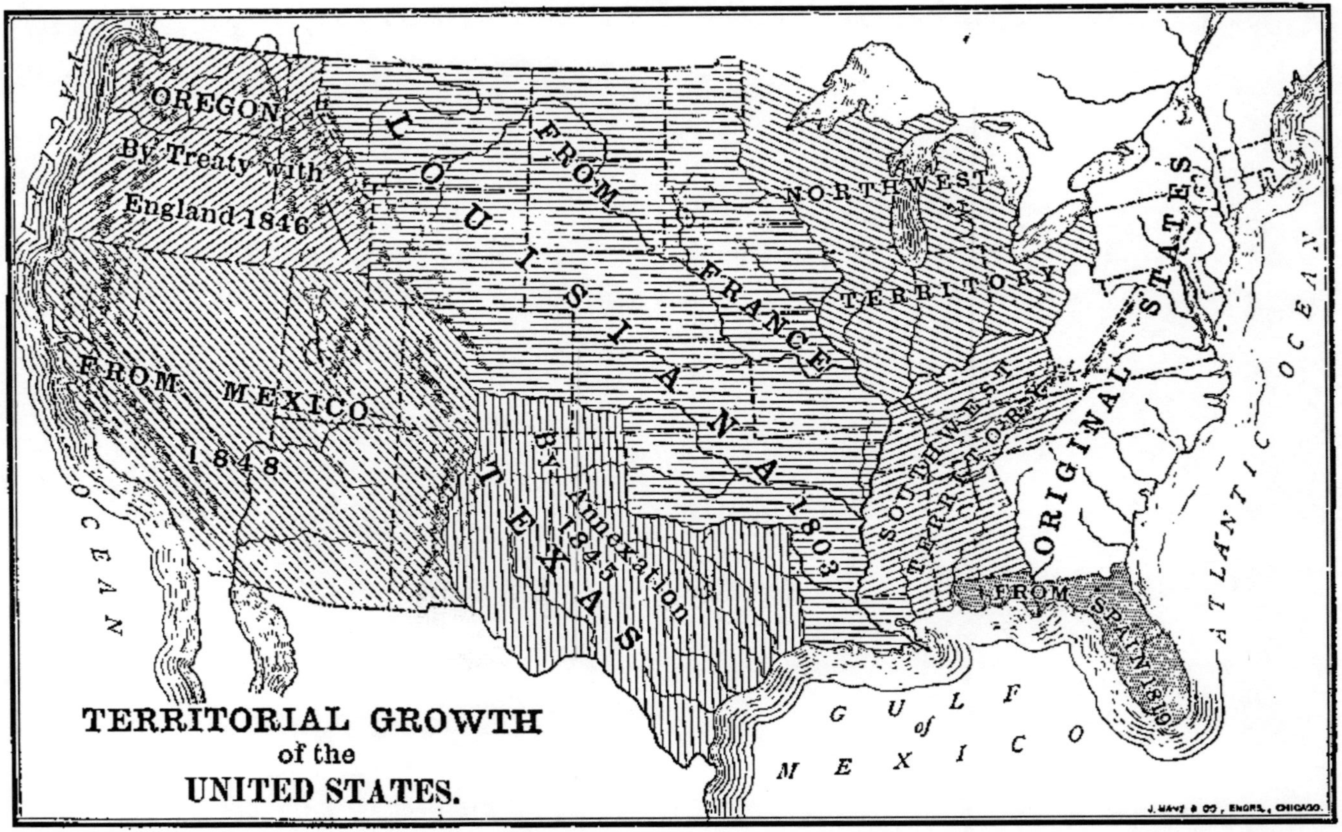

TERRITORIAL GROWTH
of the
UNITED STATES.

ATLANTIC OCEAN

ORIGINAL STATES

FROM SPAIN 1819

GULF OF MEXICO

MEXICO

NORTHWEST TERRITORY

SOUTHWEST TERRITORY

FROM FRANCE

LOUISIANA 1803

TEXAS

By Annexation 1845

OREGON
By Treaty with England 1846

FROM MEXICO
1848

PACIFIC OCEAN

J. MANZ & CO., ENGRS., CHICAGO.

The Republican Party.—A new party, the Republican by name, was organized, based upon the principle of opposition to the extension of slavery. In the Presidential election of 1856, in which John C. Fremont was the Republican candidate, and James Buchanan the Democratic nominee, the subject of slavery was, for the first time, made an issue between the opposing parties.

By the Dred Scott decision the "Missouri Compromise" was declared unconstitutional, that slaves could be held in any territory; and that slave owners could take their slaves into any state in the Union without losing their right of property in such persons.

Kansas Troubles.—As by the Kansas-Nebraska bill these territories were open to slavery if the inhabitants should so decide, free-soil men from the North flocked to settle Kansas and thus *vote* out slavery. The South also sent its representatives and war raged between the free-soil and pro-slavery settlers.

Both presidents, Pierce and Buchanan, took the part of the pro-slavery party in Kansas; but the final result was that Kansas came into the Union as a free state. The Kansas struggle was but the picket firing preluding the great national strife.

The Sumner Outrage.—In May, 1856, Charles Sumner, of Massachusetts, made a two-days' speech in the senate on what he called the "Crime against Kansas." This great effort so aroused the anger of the pro-slavery members and the South in general, that two days after the speech, as Mr. Sumner was quietly writing at his desk in the senate chamber, he was attacked by Preston S. Brooks, a member of the House from South Carolina, and nephew of Mr. Butler of the same state, to whom Mr. Sumner alluded when he said: "He cannot open his mouth, but out flies a blunder." The attack was so sudden that before Mr. Sumner could rise from his desk, and before his friends could come to his rescue, he became unconscious from the heavy blows upon his head, inflicted by the cane in the hands of Mr. Brooks.

The effect of this cowardly and brutal assault was to intensify the bitterness already existing between the North and the South; at the

North Mr. Sumner was defended, and resolutions and indignation meetings denouncing Mr. Brooks's action were of common occurrence.

Thus the Sumner assault became a factor in the great slavery contest of the nation.

John Brown.—Another event had a like effect upon the feelings of the people. John Brown, one of the Kansas anti-slavery settlers, conceived the idea of immediate freedom of the slaves, and gathering a small company of both black and white men, attacked the United States arsenal at Harper's Ferry. Most of his associates were killed or imprisoned, and he was captured, tried and hung by the authority of the State of Virginia. John Brown's act was generally condemned by the people of the North as well as the South, though a few considered him a martyr to freedom. Afterwards, in commemoration of the spirit of the act, the soldiers' rallying song, "John Brown's body lies mouldering in the grave, but his soul goes marching on," became famous.

Republican Party.—There had always been an anti-slavery element in both the Whig and the Democratic parties, but the Republican party was the first to declare openly against the extension of slavery. The Democratic party became the pro-slavery party. When in 1860 Abraham Lincoln was elected President the South was ripe for secession. By the long struggle outlined in the preceding pages, the South had become so frenzied in its opposition to the sentiments of the North, and the infringement upon what it considered its rights, that it was ready to follow its most extreme leaders, and the result was *secession* and *war.*

CHAPTER II.

HOW THE ARMY WAS ORGANIZED.

As we are to study a great war, it is well to know something of the organization of the army, the terms used, and the difficulties to be overcome. The Company is the smallest organized unit of the army. A Captain and two Lieutenants are the commissioned officers of the company. Ten or twelve companies form a regiment. A Colonel, a Lieutenant-Colonel, and a Major constitute the officers of a regiment. The regiment is a kind of family. To be away from the regiment meant to the soldier to be absent from home. From three to five regiments were placed in a brigade, with either a Brigadier-General or a Colonel commanding. From two to four brigades constituted a division, commanded either by a Major-General or a senior Brigadier-General. Usually three divisions formed a corps, commanded by a Major-General.

The army was not divided into corps at the beginning of the war, but as it grew in number it became necessary in order to skilfully handle so large a body of men.

Divisions of the Army.—

Army.........Commander................Senior Major-General.
Corps......... " ....Major-General.
Division...... " ....Junior Major-General.
Brigade....... " ....Brigadier-General.
Regiment..... " ....Colonel.
Company...... " ....Captain.

Needs of an Army.—An army must be fed, clothed, and sheltered as far as possible. It must have arms and ammunition. Its sick and wounded must be cared for. At the head of each department, corresponding to these needs, is an officer whose duty it is to see that the men of his command are supplied with what is necessary in his department. The Quartermaster and Commissary supply the bodily needs of the men; the Ordnance officer, the arms and ammunition and the Medical department cares for the sick and the wounded. The heads of these departments compose a part of the staff of the commanding officer.

The staff are the assistants of the commanding officer. Each has his special duties to perform. Each is held responsible for the successful execution of his specific duty.

Difficulties in Supplying an Army.—A Union or a Confederate army rarely numbered less than forty thousand men. The Army of the Potomac several times exceeded 100,000 men. It is a very difficult task to supply and manipulate so large a number of men, and at the same time to move against an enemy ever ready to defeat and destroy. Not only the men, but a vast number of animals, must be cared for. It would take at least 4,000 six-horse teams to supply an army of 100,000 men but a short distance from its "base." Besides these, the horses of the officers, artillery, and cavalry, and a long train of ambulances for the sick and wounded, must be included. These facts must be kept in mind if we would fully realize the difficulty in handling a large army. In order to be supplied, such vast bodies of men must move along navigable rivers or along railroads. The ordinary wagon train can supply an army but a few miles from its base of supplies. A knowledge of these things will make quite clear many facts of history.

Napoleon lost his great army of nearly half a million men in the Russian snows because he had moved so far away from his base of supplies. When the Russians burned Moscow, he had neither shelter nor food for his army. It will be remembered that the valleys of Lake Champlain and the Hudson river were of great importance in all the intercolonial wars, as well as in our two wars with England. Before the time of railroads these navigable waters formed the only highway by which armies could march to and fro and be supplied. The difficulty in passing that little strip of land between Lake

Champlain and the Hudson river caused the overthrow and surrender of General Burgoyne.

Home Life of a Soldier.—Does a soldier have a home? Yes, or something that takes its place. He must have a place where he can eat, rest and sleep. He must have a social life. Even amidst the constant danger and the tedious duties of camp, his is not necessarily a gloomy life. A tin plate, a tin cup, a case-knife, and a part ownership in a frying pan and kettle comprised his kitchen utensils. When the bacon fries and the coffee boils—real coffee, which the northern housewife vainly tried to imitate by the substitution of parched wheat and barley during war times—he transfers his meal from the rail fire to the table of his invention or discovery, and eats with an appetite born of labor and exposure. His dwelling house consisted of a half ownership in what "the boys" called a "dog tent," which was made from two pieces of cloth about six feet square, buttoned together, and drawn over a horizontal stick which rested on the crotched ends of two perpendicular sticks about three or four feet high. At the open end he built his fire, and dividing his house into compartments, he makes his bed of knapsack and blanket, and with his feet to the fire, sleeps the sleep of the weary. When on the march, through sun, or rain, or snow—snail like—he carries his house and furniture with him.

Much of the time the soldiers had insufficient food, and that not of a proper kind. When in camp it was often a puzzle to know how to occupy the time. Story-telling, whittling, games of all kinds, writing, reading, whenever reading matter was to be obtained, were the chief occupations, varied by mending and a little washing occasionally.

The real home was an experience of the past, or known only in the dreams of night.

Preparations for War.—At the fall of Fort Sumter the Northern people realized that war was upon them—a dread reality. Before this they could not believe that the South would resort to so extreme measures. Neither section understood the other. The impetuous South believed that the Northern people were lacking in chivalry, and would not fight; but beneath their apparent stoicism burned the fires of patriotic zeal. Many of the Northern people did not favor coercing the South, and did not believe that it could be compelled by force to remain in the Union. "Let the erring sisters go" was their advice.

Mr. Lincoln in his inaugural address said that he had no intention of interfering with slavery in the states; but he also declared that no state could lawfully withdraw from the Union; and that his official power should be used "To hold, occupy and possess the property and places belonging to the Government."

This meant war should the Southern states persist in their efforts to secede.

When Mr. Lincoln called for troops to put down the rebellion, Senator Stephen A. Douglas, of Illinois, loyally came forward to the support of Mr. Lincoln in his efforts to save the Union. The extra session of Congress called by President Lincoln met on the 4th of July, and by this time, so prompt was the response to the call for troops, the Union army had grown to more than 250,000 strong, mostly three-year volunteers. The South was just as prompt to respond to the call of the Confederate authorities.

Why the South was Better Prepared.—At the beginning the South was much better prepared for war than the North. The Southern people were more military in their tastes and training. The arsenals and navy yards in the South were all seized by the Confederate authorities. The great naval station at Portsmouth, near Norfolk, Virginia, was abandoned after most of the numerous vessels of war stationed there had been sunk. The United States arsenal at Harper's Ferry was burned to prevent its falling into the hands of Virginia secessionists. Immense stores of small arms, cannon, foundries and large quantities of powder fell into the hands of Southern forces.

President Buchanan's Secretary of War, Floyd, had managed to have most of the arms stored in Southern arsenals so that the North had but one arsenal left, that at Springfield, Massachusetts.

Strength of the North.—The North was much stronger in men and *general* resources, but slower to act. The South being an agricultural community, sold its cotton, sugar and tobacco to Europe, purchasing in return such manufactured articles as it needed. The North was full of teeming work-shops; the Northwest a vast store house of food products and mineral resources. Soon after the firing on Sumter, President Lincoln proclaimed a blockade on Southern ports which, if successfully accomplished, would prove a heavy blow to the South, as it depended on Europe for many things necessary for its convenience.

Hopes of the South.—On the other hand, England and France must have the cotton from the South to keep their looms going. For this very reason the South hoped that these two nations would acknowledge the Confederacy as an independent government, and furnish them aid in the contest.

"Cotton is king" was the cry of the Confederacy, and its hopes of recognition and aid continued until the last year of the war.

While England and France did not acknowledge the Confederate states as a nation, they did recognize it as a belligerent power entitled to all the rights of war.

There was great suffering among the manufacturing classes of England on account of the scarcity of cotton, but they were loyal to the free North, while the upper classes were outspoken in favor of the South.

CHAPTER III.

—

MILITARY EVENTS OF 1861.

Within a few hours after the first call for troops by President Lincoln, regiments from Massachusetts, New York and Pennsylvania were on their way to Washington.

On the morning of the 19th of April, the anniversary of the battle of Lexington, a Massachusetts regiment reached Baltimore. Here it was attacked by a mob incited by Southern sympathizers in the city. Several were killed on both sides, and the regiment after much difficulty was able to take the cars for Washington. For several days no troops were permitted to pass through Baltimore for the relief of Washington. But General Butler with the Massachusetts 6th regiment, and Colonel Lefferts with the New York 7th, passed down Chesapeake Bay to Annapolis. From here, repairing the railroad as they went, they marched overland to Washington. General Butler soon after took possession of Baltimore. Union troops now pouring through the city gathered at Washington, securing it from immediate danger.

Fortress Monroe, between the James and the York rivers, commanding the entrance to the Chesapeake Bay, was still occupied by the United States troops, but was at this time in danger of falling into the hands of the Confederate troops gathering about it. General Butler with a large force was sent to reinforce it.

West Virginia.—A large majority of the people of West Virginia remained loyal to the Union, and refused to follow the remainder of the state in its secession. This section set up a government of its own, which was afterward admitted as a state. The seat of the Confederate government was removed from Montgomery, Alabama, to Richmond, Virginia, necessarily making that part of Virginia between the capitals the principal battle-ground of the war.

General George B. McClellan had command of the Department of the Ohio. General W. S. Rosecrans commanded in West Virginia under him. By the close of July, 1861, the Confederate forces were all driven out of West Virginia, being defeated at the battles of Rich Mountain, Cheat River and Carrick's Ford.

Bull Run.—By the last of June a force of 40,000 men had gathered in the vicinity of Washington. The Union troops had taken possession of Arlington Heights in Virginia, opposite Washington, this being the home of General R. E. Lee, of the Confederate army. This position and Alexandria further down the river were strongly fortified. The Northern people became impatient at what they considered unnecessary delay, and their cry was "On to Richmond." They did not understand that 40,000 undisciplined men hurriedly brought together do not constitute an army. It takes much time to produce an effective army. General Winfield Scott, a general of the war of 1812, who also led our troops to victory in Mexico, was still Commander-in-chief of the Union army. Being too old and infirm to command troops in the field, General McDowell was given command of forces to move against the Confederates stationed behind Bull Run. The battle of Bull Run was fought July 21st. At first the Union troops were successful, and up to four o'clock in the afternoon all seemed to be in their favor, but a panic seized them, and a large part of the army fled in confusion to Washington. This disaster was a severe blow to the pride of the North, but it taught a lesson that had to be learned, that this war was to be no holiday affair. Immediately the North began to prepare for a long and bloody war.

General McClellan was given the command of the Army of the Potomac. Money was voted by Congress to carry on the war. Half a million men responded to the call of the President, but it took time to arm and discipline these troops, and Washington must be strongly fortified. This was the work of the east during the remainder of the year 1861.

Missouri.—The Legislature of Missouri was loyal to the Union, but its Governor made every effort to carry the state to the Confederate side. He called for 50,000 troops to drive out the "invaders," they being the loyal Missourians who had taken up arms for the Union.

General Lyon did not wait for the Confederates to organize, but drove Governor Jackson from Jefferson City, routing his forces at Boonville. In August General Lyon attacked the Confederates at Wilson's Creek, a few miles south of Springfield. Here General Lyon was killed and the Union forces driven back.

About this time General John C. Fremont was placed in command of all the Union forces in Missouri. Early in September, Colonel Mulligan was besieged at Lexington, Missouri, by a large Confederate force. After a long struggle he was compelled to surrender his force of about 2,500 men. But before the close of the year the Confederates under General Price were driven from the state. In November General Grant fought his first battle of the war at Belmont, in Missouri, opposite Columbus, Kentucky. During most of the war a large part of Missouri was in a very lawless, unsettled state. The Confederates were unable to hold possession of any part of it for any great length of time, but made frequent incursions, annoying the people and keeping many Union troops on the defensive.

This condition of affairs continued until the last year of the war, the Confederacy making periodic invasions into the state.

As the operations in Missouri lay outside the general course of events that led to the overthrow of the Confederacy, it will not be necessary to again refer to this section, though many important events transpired here, which, at other times, would be of great interest were they not overshadowed by operations of greater importance in other directions.

Events Along the Coast.—In August of this year, a naval expedition under General Burnside captured Hatteras Inlet, leading into Pamlico Sound. By this success the North got possession of all that part of the coast of North Carolina. This aided the blockade and furthered future operations in that region.

A second expedition captured Port Royal on the coast of South Carolina.

Hilton Head, on this harbor, became an important centre for naval operations on the South Atlantic coast.

Kentucky.—Kentucky was loyal to the Union, though its Governor made every effort to keep the state in a neutral position. But in September the Confederates took possession of Columbus, on the Mississippi River, while the Union troops under General Grant occupied Paducah, at the mouth of the Tennessee river. Later the Confederates occupied Bowling Green and Mill Springs. The Union troops under General D. C. Buell occupied the northern part of the state. All the events of the year 1861, both East and West, were but preliminaries to the greater struggle of following years.

There were no studied plans or campaigns. It was a time of preparation. Each side had to create its army from men who knew comparatively nothing of war. The officers of the regular army were the nucleus around which each side formed its army. Most of the officers from the South resigned their commissions in the regular army and joined the Confederate army. There were, however, some notable exceptions. General Scott and General George H. Thomas were Virginians, Admiral Farragut was a Tennesseean, while other Southerners of less note remained devoted to the Union.

The Trent Affair.—Captain Wilkes of the United States navy intercepted the British ship "Trent," which had on board two Confederate commissioners on their way to England and France to invite sympathy and aid. These he took prisoners and came near involving us in war with England. This was considered an insult to the British flag, but a conflict was avoided by compliance to the demand of England to give up the prisoners.

Summary of 1861.—1. Secession of South Carolina and Gulf states. (Jan., 1861.)

2. Confederate Government located at Montgomery, Ala. (Feb. 4th, 1861.)

3. Mr. Lincoln inaugurated President. (March 4th, 1861.)

4. Surrender of Fort Sumter. (April 14th.)

5. Call for troops. (April 15th.)
6. Secession of other Southern states.
7. Capture of forts and arsenals by Confederates. (April.)
8. Removal of Confederate capital to Richmond.
9. Extra session of Congress. (July 4th.)
10. Baltimore riot. (April 19th.)
11. Confederates driven from West Virginia.
12. Bull Run. Confederate victory. (July 21st.)
13. General McClellan made commander of the Union army. Ball's Bluff. (October 21st.)
14. Roanoke Island and Port Royal Harbor captured. Union victory. (November 27th.)
15. In Missouri—Wilson's Creek. (August 10th.) Death of General Lyon, August 10th. General Fremont in command. Battle of Belmont. (Nov. 7th.)
16. Kentucky occupied by Union and Confederate troops.
17. Trent affair. (November 8th.)

—

EXERCISE ON MAP II.

Map II represents the field of operations in the West for 1862-63 and 1864.

Locate St. Louis, Cairo, Paducah, Louisville, Cincinnati, Bowling Green, Perryville, Frankfort, Mill Spring, Belmont, Columbus, Fort Henry, Fort Donelson, Nashville, Franklin, Island No. 10, Fort Pillow, Memphis, Pittsburg Landing (or Shiloh), Corinth, Florence, Decatur, Chattanooga, Knoxville, Murfreesboro.

Trace the railroad from Louisville to Atlanta, through Nashville and Chattanooga.

Trace the Tennessee river from Paducah to Knoxville.

Trace the Mississippi river from St. Louis to its mouth.

Study location of all the rivers south of Tennessee.

All named or numbered on the map should be fixed in the mind.

MAP II

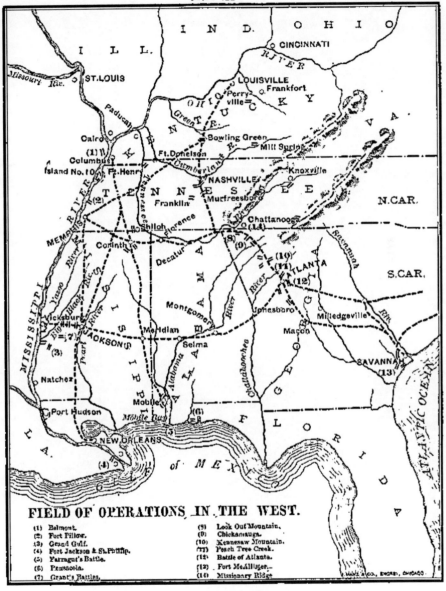

FIELD OF OPERATIONS IN THE WEST.

(1) Belmont.
(2) Fort Pillow.
(3) Grand Gulf.
(4) Fort Jackson & St. Phillip.
(5) Farragut's Battle.
(6) Pensacola.
(7) Grant's Battles.
(8) Look Out Mountain.
(9) Chickamauga.
(10) Kennesaw Mountain.
(11) Peach Tree Creek.
(12) Battle of Atlanta.
(13) Fort McAllister.
(14) Missionary Ridge

CHAPTER IV.

EVENTS IN THE WEST, 1862.

The first object to be accomplished by the Union army in the West was to gain possession of the Mississippi river. If this could be done, the Confederate territory would be cut in two, and the overthrow of the Confederacy only a question of time. The South realizing this, strongly fortified the river at different points from Columbus to its mouth.

The second object was to get possession of Kentucky, Tennessee and Georgia. The destruction of the Confederate army was, of course, the final result to be accomplished, but this could not be reasonably hoped for until the resources of the South were crippled, and the country so divided as to make it impossible to sustain the armies in the field. From the nature of the case, the Union armies must act on the "offensive," that is, must drive the Confederates before them. Should the South be able to retain possession of its own territory, or a considerable part of it, success would ultimately crown its efforts.

The North in order to succeed must move forward, and occupy the strongholds of the South.

Commanders and Positions.—During the winter of 1861–62 in the West, General H. W. Halleck commanded along the Mississippi river and in Missouri, with headquarters at St. Louis.

General Grant under him commanded at Cairo, Ill., and Paducah. General D. C. Buell commanded in Kentucky, with headquarters at Louisville. Commodore Foote commanded the rivers. The flotilla of gunboats had much to do with the opening of the Mississippi river.

The Confederate line extended from Columbus on the Mississippi river, through Fort Henry on the Tennessee river, Fort Donelson on

the Cumberland, and Bowling Green south of Greene river, to Mi
Spring on the upper course of the Cumberland river. The positio
at Columbus was so strong that it could not well be taken by th
Union forces, so the Confederate line must be broken at some othe
point. The Tennessee river being navigable for steamboats up as fa
as Florence, Alabama, and the Cumberland to Nashville and beyond
the Union army had the choice of four lines of advance, each d
fended by a Confederate force.

First, by the Mississippi river defended at Columbus; second, b
the Tennessee river defended at Fort Henry; third, by the Cumber
land river defended at Fort Donelson; fourth, by the Louisville an
Nashville railroad defended at Bowling Green. The first and fourt
positions were very strong, the second and third on the Tennesse
and Cumberland rivers being the weaker points of the Confederat
line.

EXERCISE ON MAP III.

(1), (2), (3), (4) and (5) represent five places held by the Con
federates, and is their line of defense January 1, 1862.

Name them.

The shaded part represents states held by Confederates at sam
date.

Name them.

Why do the Confederates occupy (1), (2), (3), (4)?

What would be the effect should the Union forces take (2) or (3)

Suppose a Union army with gunboats were at No. (6), and a Con
federate army at (4), what would be the effect?

Union troops occupy (8), (9) and (10): Name the places.

Broken lines represent railroads (– – – – – – – –).

Why, then, is Bowling Green held by the Confederates?

No. (2) is the weakest point in the Confederate line; how strong
then, is the Confederate line?

How much of the Mississippi river do the Confederates now hold

Why was it necessary first to take Chattanooga before East Ten
nessee could be permanently occupied by Union army?

MAP III

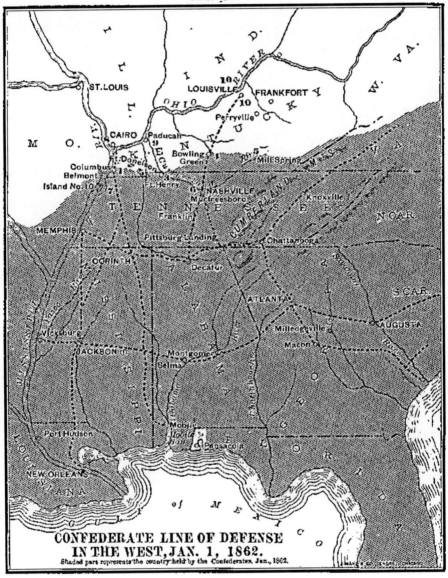

**CONFEDERATE LINE OF DEFENSE
IN THE WEST, JAN. 1, 1862.**

Shaded part represents the country held by the Confederates, Jan., 1862.

Mill Springs, Fort Henry and Donelson.—Early in the spring General George H. Thomas was sent to Mill Springs, where he defeated the Confederates, thus driving back their "right wing." Early in February General Grant's forces and the gunboats under Commodore Foote were sent against Fort Henry on the Tennessee river. This being quickly taken, the Tennessee river was now open to the Union army and gunboats as far as Northern Alabama. After taking Fort Henry, General Grant marched his troops across the narrow neck of land lying between the two rivers and besieged Fort Donelson. Here the gunboats in attempting to take the fort were defeated. But the Union army invested the fort, and after some very heavy fighting captured it with about 15,000 prisoners.

It was at this place that General Grant got the title "Unconditional Surrender" (U. S.) Grant.

When the Confederate commander asked for "terms," General Grant's reply was: "No terms except unconditional and immediate surrender can be accepted. I propose to move immediately upon your works."

This victory enabled the army and gunboats to pass up the Cumberland river to Nashville, thus placing the Union army south of Bowling Green and the Confederate army, should it remain there, but it did not.

By getting possession of these two rivers, the Confederate "line of defense," in military language, was broken.

General Albert Sidney Johnston, commanding at Bowling Green, withdrew his army through Nashville to Corinth, in Northern Mississippi, thus placing his army south of the Tennessee as well as the Cumberland river. By the capture of these two forts the Confederate line was driven two hundred miles south. The Confederates at Columbus withdrew to Island No. 10. A few weeks later this place, with a large number of prisoners, was captured by General John Pope and Commodore Foote, the Confederates falling back to Fort Pillow, near Memphis, Tennessee.

The three victories of Fort Henry, Fort Donelson and Island No. 10, advanced the Union lines so as to include all of Kentucky, Middle and Western Tennessee.

The Confederate line of defense now extended from Memphis, Tennessee, through Corinth, Mississippi, along the Tennessee river to Chattanooga.

General Halleck at St. Louis was now given command of all the troops in the Mississippi valley, which brought General Buell under his command.

General Buell, commanding the Union army in Kentucky, followed General Johnston through Nashville and took possession of Central Tennessee.

General Grant moved his army up the Tennessee river to Pittsburg Landing, near Corinth.

General Halleck ordered General Buell to march across the country and join General Grant at Pittsburg Landing. The two armies were to attack Corinth, where General Johnston had concentrated his forces. General Halleck now had command of three armies: the Army of the Ohio, afterwards called the Army of the Cumberland, under General D. C. Buell; the Army of the Tennessee, under the command of Gen. U. S. Grant, and the Army of the Mississippi, under General John Pope. The last army soon lost its name, becoming a part of the Army of the Tennessee.

General Halleck · had a fourth army under him in Missouri, but not directly connected with the operations along the Mississippi river.

Battle of Pittsburg Landing, or Shiloh.—Up to this time the Union army had taken the "offensive," and the Confederates now determined to "strike back".

Knowing that General Buell was marching from Nashville to join General Grant at Pittsburg Landing, the Confederate commanders, Johnston and Beauregard, sought to defeat General Grant's forces before General Buell could come to their aid.

On the morning of April 6th, 1862, the Confederate army attacked the Union army with great force and bravery. All day the battle raged. The Union army fought bravely and desperately, but it was gradually driven back toward the Tennessee river, until at nightfall it formed a line near the river. One more retreat and it would have been swallowed by the river. The Confederates, although so far successful, were greatly fatigued, and had lost their commander, General A. S. Johnston. That night General Buell's army crossed the Tennessee river to join in the battle of the next day. The second day the Confederates, now commanded by Beauregard, were steadily driven back until afternoon, when they finally gave way and found refuge in Corinth.

The losses in killed and wounded in both armies were about twenty thousand, nearly equally divided, though the Union army lost more prisoners.

Siege of Corinth.—Soon after the battle, General Halleck himself came to Pittsburg Landing, and ordered the army under General Pope, now operating on the Mississippi river, to come around by boats. These three armies now made a force of over a hundred thousand men, and so slowly did they move towards Corinth that they covered only thirty miles in the whole month of May. The Confederates evacuated Corinth and retreated south. The Confederates on the Mississippi river gave up Fort Pillow, and after a gunboat fight near Memphis, in which the Confederate gunboats were all destroyed, all retreated south to Vicksburg, Miss.

EXERCISE ON MAP IV.

The shaded part represents the country held by the Confederates April 1, 1862.

Compare this with Map III.

Confederates now hold Fort Pillow, above Memphis, Corinth and Chattanooga, with the main army under General A. S. Johnston at Corinth.

The Union army, under General Grant, occupied Pittsburg Landing on the Tennessee river, near Corinth, and is supplied by way of the Tennessee river.

Steamboats can go to Florence only.

Thus the Confederate line extends from Memphis to Chattanooga, with the Tennessee river as its line of defense.

What has the Union army gained during February and March?

It was General Johnston's main object to hold possession of the Mississippi river. That being the condition, why did he fall back so far south, from Bowling Green to Corinth?

Why did he not remain near Nashville?

General Buell marched from Nashville to Pittsburg Landing across what state?

While waiting for General Buell, General Grant was attacked by General Johnston from Corinth.

What did the Confederates thus hope to do?

How much of the Mississippi river do the Confederates still hold (April 1)?

Farragut's Operations at the Mississippi River.—While the efforts to open the Mississippi were in progress at the north, Admiral Farragut was working his way up from the south. Forts Jackson and St. Philip guarded the river below New Orleans. Between these two forts the Confederates had stretched across the river an immense chain sustained by old vessels securely anchored in the river. Above were the Confederate gunboats and fire-rafts ready to attack, should Farragut succeed in passing these obstructions. Having succeeded

MAP IV

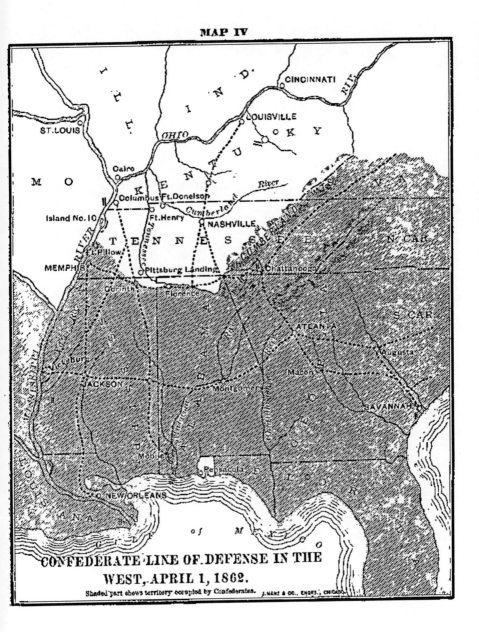

CONFEDERATE LINE OF DEFENSE IN THE WEST, APRIL 1, 1862.

Shaded part shows territory occupied by Confederates. J. WANT & CO., ENGRS., CHICAGO

in breaking the chain in the darkness of the night, early in the morning of April 24th, Farragut pushed boldly through the opening with his fleet, amidst the heavy firing of the two forts and the Confederate gunboats. Great fire-rafts were pushed against his vessels, with the purpose of setting them on fire.

After three hours of terrible fighting, all but three of Farragut's gunboats passed the obstacles, and totally destroyed the enemy's gunboats.

General Sherman says: "No bolder or more successful act of war was ever done than this." A few days later the forts surrendered, and General Butler, with a land force, passed up the river and occupied New Orleans.

This closed all offensive operations of the Union troops in the West until late in the year. The Confederate line after leaving Memphis extended from Vicksburg on the Mississippi river, along the Tennessee river through Chattanooga.

By the last of June all of the Mississippi river was in the hands of the North, except that portion lying between Vicksburg and Port Hudson.

East Tennessee was loyal to the Union, though unfortunately that part of the state was controlled by the Confederates until the summer of 1863.

Confederates Take the Offensive.—Owing to the failure of McClellan's Peninsula campaign in the East, General Halleck was called east to take command of all the Union forces. General Pope was assigned the command of the forces in Northern Virginia, General Grant was left in command of Western Tennessee, while General Buell went to the defense of Central Tennessee. The Confederates now took the offensive in all directions, their object being to regain what they had lost in Tennessee and Kentucky.

Perryville.—General Bragg was sent with a large Confederate force to Chattanooga and Central Tennessee. From here he invaded Kentucky, where he met another Confederate force from East Tennessee. It now became a foot-race between the Union and the Confederate armies as to which should reach Louisville first. General

Buell was a little ahead. After being reinforced, he turned on General Bragg, and at the battle of Perryville defeated him.

General Bragg now fell back to Murfreesboro in Central Tennessee, where he remained until driven south later in the year.

Iuka and Corinth.—The Southern army was also active in Western Tennessee. A force in attempting to reach Central Tennessee was defeated by Generals Grant and Rosecrans at Iuka.

Soon after a large Confederate force attempted to retake Corinth, but met with a very disastrous defeat by the Union troops under the command of General Rosecrans. This closed all the *offensive* operations of the Confederates in the West for this year.

The Government at Washington being displeased with the conduct of General Buell in his operations against General Bragg, relieved him from the command of the Army of the Cumberland, and placed it in the hands of General W. S. Rosecrans.

Stone River.—During the last days of the year 1862 and the first of January, 1863, the offensive was again renewed by the Union army, and the desperate battle of Stone River, or Murfreesboro, was fought, which resulted in the retreat of General Bragg to the south, General Bragg leaving most of Central Tennessee in the possession of the Union army. In this battle over 23,000 men were lost, the losses on both sides being nearly equal. This closed the operations of the West for the year 1862.

EXERCISE ON MAP V.

AT THE CLOSE OF 1862.

What part of the Mississippi river was held by the Confederates at the close of the year 1862?

Compare this map with No. IV, also with No. III.

Battles or sieges are marked by parallel lines (===).

All in the unshaded part represent battles fought in 1862.

How many are there? Name them.

Why was there a battle so far north as Perryville?

Notice the unshaded part at the mouth of the Mississippi river.

What event opened that part of the river?

MAP V

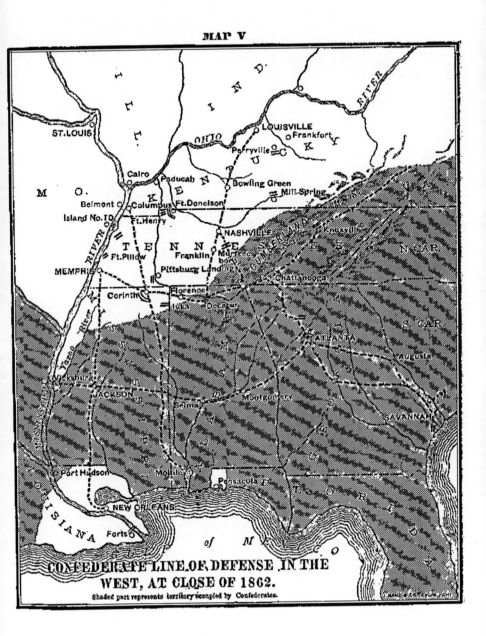

CONFEDERATE LINE OF DEFENSE IN THE WEST, AT CLOSE OF 1862.

Shaded part represents territory occupied by Confederates.

REVIEW OF 1862 IN THE WEST.

OFFENSIVE OPERATIONS OF THE UNION ARMY—ALL UNION VICTORIES

Mill Spring (January).
Fort Henry (February 6th).
Fort Donelson (February 16th).
Island No. 10 (April 7th).
Farragut's passing the forts (April 24th to 28th).
Capture of New Orleans (May 1st).
Siege of Corinth (evacuated in the latter part of May).
Fort Pillow and Memphis (evacuated June 4th).
Stone River (December 1862 and January, 1863).

Result: Union forces occupy all the Mississippi river except the portion between Vicksburg and Port Hudson, and all of Kentucky and Central Tennessee.

ON THE DEFENSIVE—ALL UNION VICTORIES.

Shiloh (April 6–7).
Iuka (September 19th).
Corinth.

All territory gained the first of the year remained in possession of Union troops.

CHAPTER V.

WAR IN THE EAST—1862.

A Study of Virginia.—The operations in the West covered a very large area of country, extending from the Ohio river on the north to the Gulf of Mexico on the south, and from Missouri to the Carolinas. In the East the war was confined to a much smaller space. Gettysburg in the North and Appomattox in the South mark the northern and southern extremes of the battlefields in this region. Virginia offered peculiar advantages both to the North and to the South.

Advantages to the North.—The Chesapeake Bay on the east, with

for some distance. The North, having complete command of these waters, could transport its armies and munitions of war to any part of the eastern coast of Virginia.

Advantages to the South.—On the other hand, the South had many advantages over the North in geographical position. The many streams flowing southeast across the state were lines of defense for the Confederate army. In times of war, rivers and mountains are used, when possible, as means of defense against an enemy. It is very difficult, and many times impossible, for an army to cross a river or a mountain in the face of an enemy. In such cases it becomes necessary to "flank" an enemy, this being a military term meaning to go around, in order to get past an enemy's strong position.

The Shenandoah Valley.—The fertile Shenandoah Valley, through which flows the river of the same name, supplied the Confederate army while passing through it. This valley, protected by nature's wall, the Blue Ridge Mountains, was an open highway to the North, and so completely might the Confederates be shielded by this wall of protection as to render them almost safe from an attack from the direction of Washington.

The Confederates were quick to see the advantages of this position, and to avail themselves of the favorable circumstances. This valley became the scene of many brilliant exploits, first by the Confederate General Stonewall Jackson and later by General P. H. Sheridan of the Union army.

The Routes to Richmond.—In the spring of 1862, when the time came to move the Army of the Potomac, the question was, " What route shall be taken to Richmond?"

There were four lines of advance by which the Union army could be supplied while moving from Washington upon the Confederate capital.

The first was along the railroad through Gordonsville ; the second was by the way of the Potomac river and Fredericksburg by R. R. to Richmond ; third by Chesapeake Bay, up the York river, then by a short railroad to Richmond ; the fourth by Chesapeake Bay and James river.

By the first the army would protect Washington at the same time it was operating against the enemy, but this was the longest route, as well as the one most difficult to guard.

The third and fourth, by the way of the Peninsula, made it very easy to supply the army by either the York or the James rivers, but left Washington open to attack from a wide-awake enemy. The second line was probably the best one to take, but the difficulty was that the Confederate army stood in the way of any route.

A difference of opinion as to the best route arose between President Lincoln and General McClellan. The president wished the army to move directly against the enemy along the railroad, his idea being that the same army must be met upon any road. General McClellan wished to move by one of the other lines, and the President finally yielded upon the condition that a sufficient force should be left to guard Washington.

As these two men afterward became opposing candidates for the Presidency, this question became a political one, and much feeling arose in its discussion.

EXERCISE ON MAP VI.

VIRGINIA.

Into what water and in what direction does each river of Virginia flow?

What direction is Washington from Richmond?

Gettysburg from Washington?

Shenandoah Valley from Washington?

Bull Run from Washington?

Baltimore from Washington?

Petersburg from Richmond?

Yorktown from Richmond?

General McClellan took his army down the Potomac river and Chesapeake Bay, up the York river to White House, then toward Richmond across the Chickahominy.

Trace his route.

General Lee in both invasions marched from south of the Rapidan into and down the Shenandoah Valley, crossing the Potomac into Maryland, the Union army keeping between him and Washington.

Trace his route.

What advantage was it for him to be in the valley?

General Grant's army faced westward in nearly all the battles he fought in Virginia. Why?

Locate everything named or numbered on the map.

Note the two belts of battlefields:

I.   From Gettysburg to New Market.

II.   From Bull Run to Five Forks.

Name the battlefields in order in each of these two red belts of war. Do you think of any reasons why these battlefields should be so located?

MAP VI

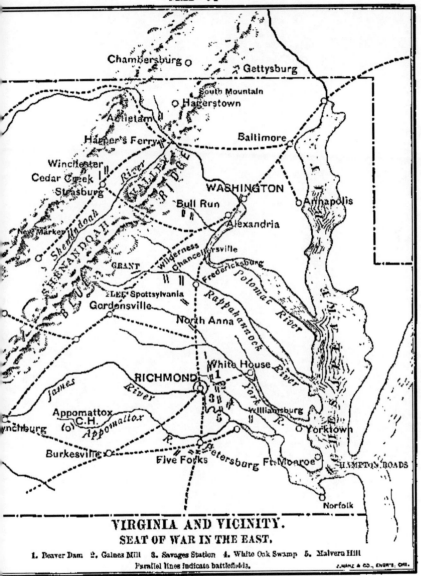

VIRGINIA AND VICINITY.
SEAT OF WAR IN THE EAST.

1. Beaver Dam 2. Gaines Mill 3. Savages Station 4. White Oak Swamp 5. Malvern Hill
Parallel lines indicate battlefields.

J. MANZ & CO., ENGR'S. CHI.

The Merrimac and Monitor.—A short time before General Mc-Clellan started on his Peninsular campaign, an event occurred which caused a revolution in the navies of the world. This was the fight between the Merrimac and the Monitor in Hampton Roads, near Fortress Monroe. The Confederates had taken the Merrimac, a United States war vessel that had fallen into their hands at the time Norfolk was abandoned, and converted her into an iron-clad vessel, with an iron prow, and armed her with the heaviest guns. All this made her a very formidable, shot-proof, steam monster.

On the morning of March 8th, she moved out to attack the Union fleet lying at Hampton Roads. She sunk the Cumberland, captured the Congress, and scattered the rest of the fleet. The heaviest shot of the Union guns seemed to have no effect upon her armor. But during the night the " Yankee cheese-box on a raft," as the Monitor was called, arrived from New York. This was the first turreted iron-clad ever built, and the next morning she had the opportunity of trying her power.

Soon the Merrimac moved out, expecting to complete the destruction of the Union fleet. The little giant met the monster, but the guns of neither seemed to have any effect upon the other, and the Merrimac withdrew to her former position.

Two months later the Merrimac was destroyed by the Confederates when they abandoned Norfolk.

The Peninsular Campaign.—General McClellan in May transferred his army from Washington by water to the mouth of the York river.

At Yorktown he found a Confederate force intrenched across his path. After holding the Union army in check at this place for several weeks, the Confederates fell back towards Richmond. The Union army overtook them at Williamsburg, when a severe but indecisive battle was fought.

General McClellan gradually advanced his army toward Richmond, and extended his right wing to the north as far as Mechanicsville, and his left south of the Chickahominy river. The army was thus cut in two by this stream. The Confederate commander, General Joseph E. Johnston, taking advantage of a heavy rainstorm, which caused this river to overflow its banks and destroy its bridges, attacked that part of the army south of the river, hoping thus to destroy it before the other part could come to its aid. This he came near doing, but after two days' fighting was driven back to Richmond. This is known as the battle of Fair Oaks, or Seven Pines. General J. E. Johnston was wounded, and his command given to General Robert E. Lee.

While the Confederates were holding General McClellan in check around Richmond, General Stonewall Jackson moved rapidly north driving the Union army out of the Shenandoah Valley, and causing great alarm for the safety of Washington. But to take Washington was not in his plans. He moved quickly south and joined General Lee near Richmond. With these combined forces General Lee, leaving a sufficient force in the defense of Richmond to insure its safety, moved out of Richmond and attacked General McClellan from the north.

General McClellan then moved his army to the James river, but in doing so was obliged to fight the seven days' battles of Beaver Dam, Gaines' Mill, Savage's Station, White Oak Swamp and Malvern Hill.

The Peninsular campaign was a failure, and the Confederates took the offensive by moving northward to threaten Washington.

EXERCISE ON THE MAP OF THE PENINSULAR CAMPAIGN, VII.

General McClellan moved up between the York and the Chickahominy rivers. What direction did he move?

From White House he moved toward Richmond. What direction did he take, and what stream must he cross in order to reach Richmond? How did he supply his army?

What direction did the Union army face while besieging Richmond?

General Lee attacked McClellan from the north, and Beaver Dam, Gaines' Mill, Savage's Station, White Oak Swamp and Malvern Hill were the battles fought in the order named. In what direction did McClellan retreat?

This retreat was called a "change of base." The base of supplies for the Union army had been at York river; it was now changed to what river?

MAP VII

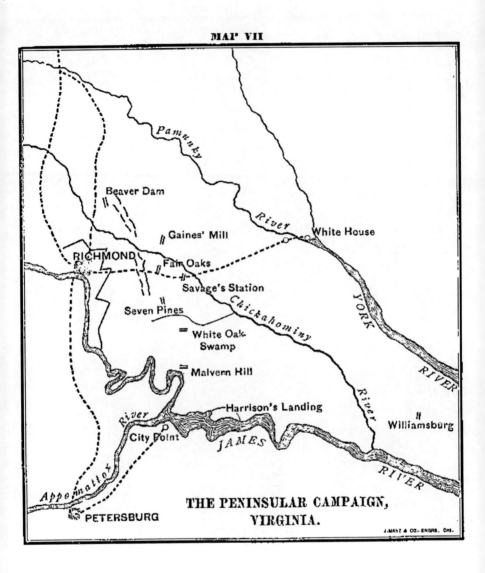

THE PENINSULAR CAMPAIGN,
VIRGINIA.

J.MANZ & CO.-ENGRS. CHI.

MAP VIII

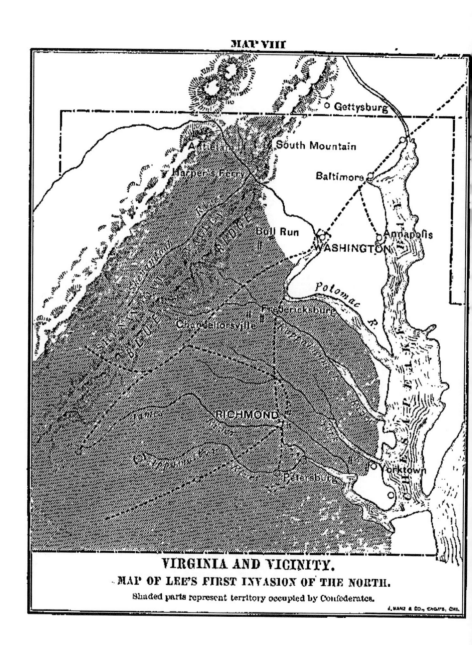

VIRGINIA AND VICINITY.
MAP OF LEE'S FIRST INVASION OF THE NORTH.

Shaded parts represent territory occupied by Confederates.

J. MANZ & CO., ENG'R'S, CHI.

Lee's First Invasion of the North.—By the middle of June the offensive operations on the part of the North had closed in the West. By the last of June the Peninsular campaign had closed in the East. The Confederates now took the offensive both in the East and West. General Halleck was called to command all the forces of the Union. General Pope was given command of the forces to defend Washington ; Stonewall Jackson was again sent north with the purpose of threatening Washington. General Lee then moved north to join General Jackson, hoping, with their combined forces, to overcome Pope before General McClellan could come to his rescue. General Jackson pushed northward, but failing to drive the Union army under General Banks, at the battle of Cedar Mountain, passed through the Shenandoah Valley, around Pope's army, and destroyed the railroad, and captured many stores at Manassas. General Pope, turning on General Jackson, attacked him near the old battleground of Bull Run. The Army of the Potomac had been withdrawn from the Peninsula to aid in the defense of Washington, and one corps of the Army of the Potomac was with General Pope in this battle. Others were near but gave no aid. The second day the remainder of Lee's forces came up, and the Union army was again defeated near the fated battlefield. This battle was Groveton, or Second Bull Run. Pope's army falling back, all the Union forces from Virginia were now concentrated at Washington, and General McClellan given the command.

General Lee moved rapidly north into Maryland, and sent General Jackson against Harper's Ferry, which he captured with 11,000 prisoners. General McClellan moved north against the Confederates, driving them from South Mountain. General Lee placed his army on the defensive behind Antietam Creek. Here was fought the very severe battle of Antietam, or, as the South called it, Sharpsburg, where the Confederates were badly defeated, and from whence they retreated south.

Soon after this General McClellan was relieved from the command of the Army of the Potomac, and General Ambrose E. Burnside placed in command. General Burnside moved the army to Fred-

ericksburg, intending to take that route to Richmond. Again t
Army of Northern Virginia was an obstruction across its path. He
in December was fought the battle of Fredericksburg. The Uni
army lost heavily and gained no advantage. Thus ends the year 18
in the East.

SYNOPSIS OF THE YEAR 1862.

In the East.—

Merrimac and Monitor—neither victorious. Merrimac finally c
   stroyed. (March 9th.)

   Peninsular Campaign.—

Offensive operations of the North.

Movement of the army to Yorktown.

Siege of Yorktown. Union victory. (Evacuated May 3d.)

Williamsburg. Union victory. (May 5th.)

Siege of Richmond. (May and June.)

   Defensive.—

Fair Oaks. Union victory. (May 31st.)

Mechanicsville. Union victory. (June 26th.)

Gaines' Mill. Confederate victory. (June 27th.)

Savage's Station. Union victory. (June 29th.)

White Oak Swamp. Confederate victory. (June 30th.)

Malvern Hill. Union victory. (July 1st.)

Final result: Peninsular campaign a failure.

   In Northern Virginia.—

Shenandoah Valley. First incursion by General Jackson. Confe
   erate victory.

Withdrawal of Union army from the Peninsula.

   Lee's First Invasion of the North.—

Cedar Mountain, indecisive. (August 9th.)

Capture of Manassas by General Jackson. (August.)

Groveton, or second Bull Run, Confederate victory. (August.)

Invasion of Maryland by Confederates. (September.)

Harper's Ferry, Confederate victory. (September 15th.)

MAP IX

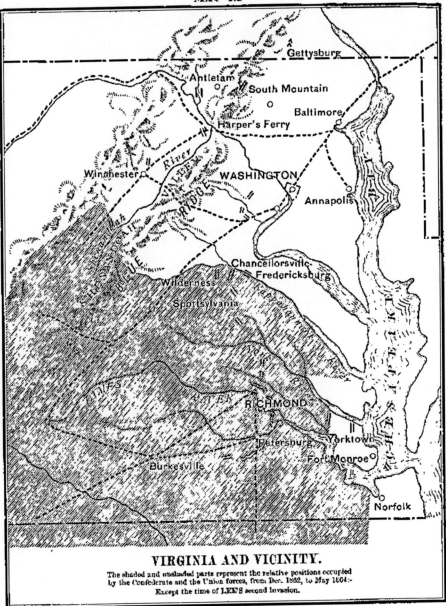

VIRGINIA AND VICINITY.

The shaded and unshaded parts represent the relative positions occupied
by the Confederate and the Union forces, from Dec. 1862, to May 1864;—
Except the time of LEE'S second invasion.

South Mountain, Union victory. (September 14th.)

Antietam, Union victory. (September 17th.)

Final result of first invasion of the North, Confederate failure.

Fredericksburg, Confederate victory. (December 13th.)

The final result of these movements and hotly contested battles, was that the two contending armies face each other in about the same position, and have about the same relative strength as at the beginning of the year.

The losses in battle were nearly equal.

The losses to the Union army by battle were probably not less than 50,000 men.

The fact that nothing had been gained in the East was practically a defeat to the North.

But taking the work of the West into account, the balance for the year was decidedly in favor of the North.

CHAPTER VI.

PREPARATIONS—NORTH, SOUTH.

Congress—In 1862 Congress passed a law authorizing the issue of United States notes, commonly called "greenbacks." These were to be used as money, taking the place of gold and silver, which had disappeared from circulation. Taxes were increased until they were very high, but even this amount was not sufficient to carry on the war. The Government was obliged to borrow large sums of money. The "greenbacks" were really a forced loan from the people. They were made "legal tender"—that is, if offered in payment for debts it was a legal offer. The creditor must take them or nothing. They became the money of the country.

In 1863 Congress passed an act creating national banks. Previous to this, the states had incorporated all the banks, and bills issued by them were local in value. There was no general currency in the United States until the issue of greenbacks and the national bank currency. This was a great improvement on the old method.

The Conscription Act.—Early in 1863 Congress passed the Conscription bill. This made all able-bodied men, citizens between the ages of 20 and 45, with few exceptions, liable to be called into the service. If drafted, a man could either supply a substitute or pay the Government $300 to obtain a substitute.

This aroused much feeling at the North, especially among the laboring classes and those opposed to the war. When a draft was made for 300,000 men, riots in different parts of the country occurred, the greatest of these being in New York city, where many lives were lost and much property destroyed.

Lincoln's Emancipation Proclamation.—On the first day of January, 1863, President Lincoln issued a proclamation of Emancipation.

He had in the September previous given notice that unless the South lay down their arms and return to their allegiance, he should declare all slaves within the Confederate lines to be free. Slavery in the United States, however, did not cease to exist until the XIII Amendment became a part of the Constitution, but the President's Proclamation did much toward making this amendment a result of the war.

In the South.—Every effort was made to increase the Southern army. Their conscription laws were much more rigid than those of the North, and the South enrolled a much larger proportion of the white population in its army than did the North. This could be more readily done as the slave population of the South was sufficient to supply the labor at home.

The Confederate government had great difficulty in supplying its army with the common necessaries. It also issued paper money as legal tender, but this became more and more valueless as the war progressed.

As a rule the Confederate army was well armed, but poorly fed and clothed.

WAR IN THE WEST—1863.

Vicksburg.—It will be remembered that at the close of 1862 the Confederates held only that part of the Mississippi river lying between Vicksburg and Port Hudson; that General Bragg had been driven from Murfreesboro during the last days of 1862 and first of 1863. Study map on page 45—the conditions in the West at the close of 1862.

General Grant, with the Army of the Tennessee, made several efforts during the winter to get past Vicksburg. Failing in this, he adopted the bold plan of running the batteries at Vicksburg with loaded transports and gunboats.

By the aid of these boats he was able to transport his army to the east bank of the Mississippi river and south of Vicksburg.

EXERCISE ON MAP X.

General Grant could not get to the east of Vicksburg from t
north. Why?

Running his boats by Vicksburg and Grand Gulf he crossed h
armies to the east of the river.

After their defeat at Port Gibson the Confederates gave up Grar
Gulf. Why?

The Black river was a protection to Grant as he passed towar
Jackson. Why?

Trace Grant's route and name battles in order.

"The movements of General Grant, which resulted in the captu
of Vicksburg," says General Sherman, "were not surpassed durir
the war, either in boldness of plan or brilliancy of execution."

General Grant, marching his army down the west bank of tl
Mississippi river below Grand Gulf, crossed to the east bank. Aft
driving the enemy from Port Gibson he moved rapidly north, usir
the Big Black river as a shield against the enemy from the directic
of Vicksburg.

After routing the enemy at Raymond he pushed for Jackso
the capital of Mississippi, from which place he drove the forces
General Johnston. Turning towards Vicksburg he moved quickl
westward to meet General Pemberton, who had come from Vicksbur
to intercept him on his way to Jackson. But General Grant was to
quick for him. At the battle of Champion Hill the Confederat
were defeated and fled to the Big Black river. After a short resis
ance here they were driven into Vicksburg, where they were shut i
only to come out as prisoners of war.

During this siege the inhabitants of the city suffered greatl
from depredations and lack of food.

During these movements the Union army lived on what
could find in the surrounding country, and was supplied from th
north of Vicksburg after the Confederates were driven into th

MAP X

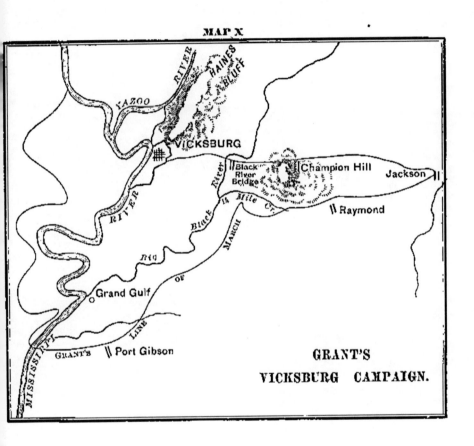

GRANT'S VICKSBURG CAMPAIGN.

city. Why did not General Grant move to the east of Vicksburg directly from the north?

During the last days of 1862, while the battle of Stone River was raging in Central Tennessee, General Sherman made an attempt to enter Vicksburg by carrying Haines' Bluff, a natural protection lying along the Yazoo river, and to the north of Vicksburg, but was unable to do so. (See map.) General Grant had during the winter made a somewhat similar attempt and failed.

The siege of Vicksburg, which began on May 18th, continued until July 4th, when General Pemberton surrendered the city with an army of over 30,000 men.

A few days later Port Hudson surrendered to General Banks, who, with his forces from New Orleans, was besieging it. This opened the Mississippi river throughout its length. The Union gunboats, aided by the strongly fortified positions at different points, effectually cut the Confederacy in two.

SYNOPSIS OF GENERAL GRANT'S MOVEMENTS.

Running the batteries of Vicksburg.
Movement of army from west to east bank.
Port Gibson.
Raymond.
Jackson.
Champion Hill.
Black River Bridge.
Siege of Vicksburg—Surrender.
Capture of Port Hudson.
Result: entire opening of Mississippi river.
Confederacy cut in two.

Chattanooga Campaign.—In June, while General Grant was besieging Vicksburg, General Rosecrans, commanding the Army of the

Cumberland in Central Tennessee, began his movements which resulted in the capture of Chattanooga. At the same time General Burnside, moving with an army from Kentucky, occupied East Tennessee. From the commencement of the war President Lincoln had been anxious to occupy this country. The people were loyal to the Union, and for that reason had suffered much at the hands of the Confederate government. By a series of successful operations General Bragg was soon driven south of the Tennessee river by General Rosecrans.

Chattanooga and Chickamauga.—Chattanooga was the military gateway to the South. She sat a queen amidst the passes of the mountains that surrounded her. The South could not afford to lose her; the North must possess her in order to penetrate further into the Confederate territory. Richmond itself was not more important to the Confederacy than was Chattanooga.

The position of this romantic as well as historic city should be well understood.

The mountains south of Chattanooga extend nearly north and south, the Tennessee river flowing nearly parallel with them. General Rosecrans crossed the river and Lookout Mountain south of Chattanooga. When General Bragg saw the Union army south of him, fearing that he might be shut in Chattanooga, he retreated south, leaving Chattanooga in the hands of the Union army. Thus far all seemed favorable to the Union army, but General Bragg, being reinforced by a corps under General Longstreet from Virginia, turned on General Rosecrans, who in his changes had allowed his forces to become too much scattered. But by rapid movements he was able to concentrate his army behind Chickamauga creek. This was for the purpose of keeping the Confederates from going back into Chattanooga. Here, during the 19th and 20th of September, was fought the desperate battle of Chickamauga, so appropriately and prophetically named by the Indians, "the River of Death." The Union troops were defeated, but were successful in holding the road to Chattanooga. During all the afternoon of the second day, after the right of the Union army had been driven back, General George H.

Thomas, with the left wing, held the enemy in check, and thus saved the Northern army from destruction. The "Rock of Chickamauga" was the title he so nobly earned in that dreadful conflict. The losses in both armies were nearly equal, total loss being about 26,000 men.

Retreating to Chattanooga, the Army of the Cumberland was followed and besieged by the Confederates; but soon a part of the Army of the Potomac, under General Hooker, was sent west to aid in holding what had been gained, viz., Chattanooga.

Changes Made.—General Grant was now made commander of all the Union troops of the West. General W. T. Sherman was given command of the Army of the Tennessee; General Rosecrans was relieved, and General Thomas was placed in command of the Army of the Cumberland.

General Sherman, with a part of the Army of the Tennessee, was brought over from Vicksburg to Chattanooga.

Battle of Chattanooga.—General Grant now had with him at Chattanooga a part of three armies. With these forces he attacked the Confederates, who were posted on Lookout Mountain and Missionary Ridge, which were on the south and east of his position. General Hooker's forces drove the Confederates from Lookout Mountain. This is sometimes called "the battle above the clouds."

General Sherman attacked the Confederates at the north end of Missionary Ridge. While all parts of the army fought equally well, it was left for the Army of the Cumberland to perform the most brilliant feat of all.

They were ordered to take the base of Missionary Ridge, but without orders, they, with heroic inspiration, charged *up the Ridge*, capturing it, and thus broke the centre of the Confederate army. The Confederates retreated to Dalton, Georgia. The victory for the Union army was complete. *The gateway to the South was open.*

While General Grant was wresting Chattanooga from the Confederates, General Longstreet, having been sent to East Tennessee, was trying to take Knoxville from the Union forces. He also was defeated. These operations left all of Tennessee in the hands of the National forces. Thus closed the events of 1863 in the West.

EXERCISE ON MAP XI.

ON CAPTURE OF CHATTANOOGA AND BATTLE OF CHICKAMAUGA.

General Rosecrans crossed his army near Bridgeport. one corp going to Chattanooga following the railroad, the second over the Raccoon, Lookout Mountain and Missionary Ridge to the valley of the Chickamauga, the third was still south of this. Where was the Union army as related to Chattanooga?

Why, then, did General Bragg leave Chattanooga?

When General Bragg turned on General Rosecrans, what was his object?

The Union army was defeated at Chickamauga and retreated to Chattanooga; what direction did it retreat?

The Confederates took possession of Lookout Point. Why could not the Union army use the railroad from Bridgeport?

EXERCISE ON MAP XI.

ON BATTLE OF CHATTANOOGA.

The words Hooker, Thomas and Sherman represent positions occupied by these Generals in the battle of Chattanooga. General Hooker moved eastward, driving the Confederates from the north end of Lookout Mountain and across the Chattanooga valley to Rossville Gap. General Sherman fought the enemy on the north end of Missionary Ridge, but could not drive them from the Ridge. While Hooker and Sherman were fighting the enemy, a part of General Thomas' army charged up the Ridge without orders, and thus broke the Confederate centre.

MAP XI

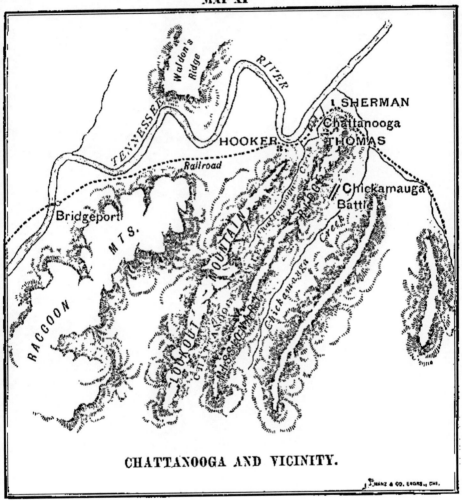

CHATTANOOGA AND VICINITY.

Synopsis of the Operations in the West, 1863.—First—Opening of the Mississippi by capture of Vicksburg, July 4th, and Port Hudson, July 8th.

Second—In Tennessee Confederates driven south of Tennessee river.

Third—East Tennessee occupied by Union troops under General Burnside.

Fourth—Occupation of Chattanooga.

Fifth—Battle of Chickamauga, Sept. 19th and 20th. 26,000 lost in both armies.

Sixth—Siege of Chattanooga by Confederates.

Seventh—Reinforcements from East and West.

Eighth—General Grant commander of all troops in the Mississippi valley.

Ninth—Battle of Chattanooga, which includes Lookout Mountain and Missionary Ridge, November 23d, 24th and 25th.

Tenth—Defeat of General Longstreet at Knoxville, Dec. 5th.

A Study of the Armies of the West.—As the two armies of the West act together from this time until the close of the war, it is well to review what they have accomplished.

Army of the Tennessee.—Its objective was to get possession of the Mississippi river. The events by which this was accomplished were: Fort Henry, Fort Donelson, Island No. 10, Pittsburg Landing, Siege of Corinth, Fort Pillow and Memphis, Iuka, battle of Corinth, campaign, siege and capture of Vicksburg.

These, with Farragut's victory and siege of Port Hudson, open the Mississippi river. It also aided in the battles which gained Chattanooga.

Commanders of the Army of the Tennessee.—General U. S. Grant, General W. T. Sherman, General J. B. McPherson, General O. O. Howard and General John A. Logan.

Army of the Cumberland.—Its objective: Occupation of Kentucky and Tennessee.

Aided in the battles of Shiloh and siege of Corinth.

Battles of Perryville, Stone River, Chickamauga and Chatta nooga.

Commanders.—General D. C. Buell (army known at this time a Army of the Ohio.)

General W. S. Rosecrans, General George H. Thomas.

EXERCISE ON MAP OF THE WEST AT THE CLOSE OF 1863

What part of Tennessee is held by the Union forces?

In what state is Chattanooga?

Does the Union army hold any part of Alabama or Georgia? If so, what part?

What part of the Mississippi river is held by Union forces?

MAP XII

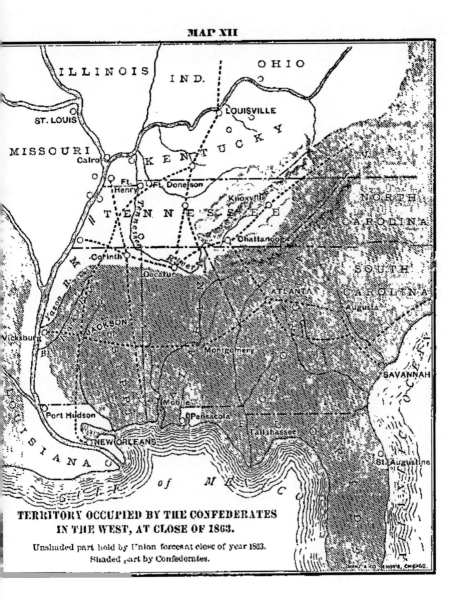

**TERRITORY OCCUPIED BY THE CONFEDERATES
IN THE WEST, AT CLOSE OF 1863.**

Unshaded part held by Union forces at close of year 1863.
Shaded part by Confederates.

CHAPTER VII.

IN THE EAST, 1863.

After the defeat of the army of the Potomac at Fredericksburg, in December, 1862, General Burnside was relieved of the command, which was given to General Joseph Hooker. Early in May, 1863, General Hooker, moving his army across the Rappahannock river, gained a position at Chancellorsville, partly in rear of the Confederate army at Fredericksburg. General Lee, not waiting to be attacked, sent a large force under Stonewall Jackson to attack the right of the Union army. This move was successful, resulting in the defeat of the Union army. General Hooker now withdrew to the north bank of the river. The Confederates won a great victory, but paid dearly for it in the death of General Jackson.

Lee's Second Invasion of the North.—About a month after the battle of Chancellorsville, General Lee started on his second northern invasion. Moving down the Shenandoah Valley he defeated the Union troops at Winchester, and crossed to the north of the Potomac.

The Union army moved parallel with the Confederates, keeping between them and Washington. General Lee moved north to Hagerstown, threatening Harrisburg, Pa.

On the 27th of June, but three days before the battle of Gettysburg, General Hooker was relieved, and General George G. Meade made commander of the Army of the Potomac.

Both armies marching northward met at Gettysburg where the first three days of July was fought one of the most desperate battles of the whole conflict. During the afternoon of July 3d, about the time that General Pemberton and General Grant were planning for the surrender of Vicksburg, General Pickett was making that most

dashing and famous but fatal charge at Gettysburg. The Confed
ates here met a crushing defeat, leaving more than a third of th
number dead, wounded, or prisoners of war on this battlefie
Confederates lost more than 25,000 men, while the Union loss w
but little less, being about 23,000.

By a study of the map it will be seen that had the Confedera
been victorious, General Lee was in a position to capture Harrisbu
Baltimore or Washington.

This is classed as one of the decisive battles of the world.
monument on the battlefield marking the farthest advance in t
famous charge of July 3d, is called the "High water-mark of t
Rebellion." After this battle General Lee retreated to Virginia,
the Shenandoah Valley, and took a stand south of the Rapidan a
Rappahannock rivers. The Union army following took its positi
north of these rivers. Aside from some minor movements duri
the fall, in which there were no positive results, the two armies
mained in these positions until the following May, at which time t
final movements of the war began.

EXERCISE ON THE MAP SHOWING LEE'S SECOND INVASION OF THE NORTH.

What direction is Gettysburg from Washington?

From Baltimore?

Compare this map with the one on page 56, representing t
first invasion.

What difference do you observe around Harper's Ferry?

In which invasion did Lee go farthest north?

Notice the Blue Ridge Mountains; what part did they play
both these invasions?

Would it have been possible for Lee to get north of Washingt
had these mountains not been there?

MAP XIII

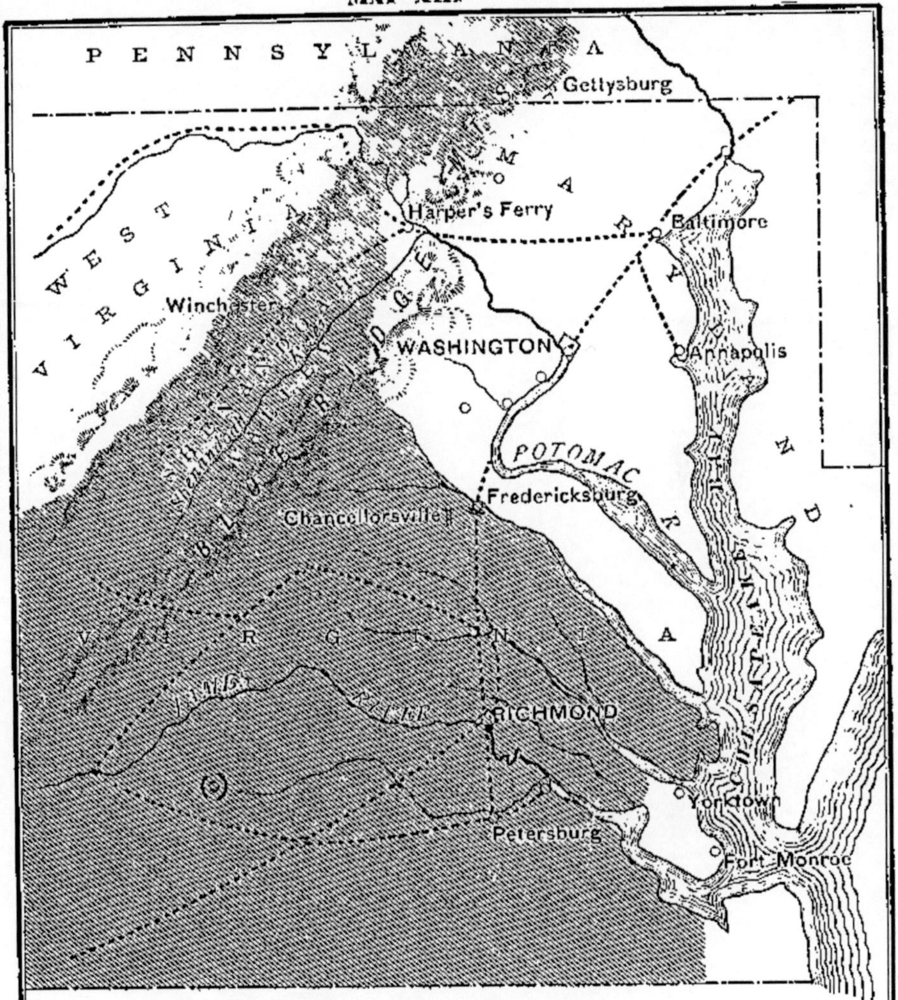
PENNSYLVANIA
Gettysburg
MARYLAND
Harper's Ferry
Baltimore
WEST VIRGINIA
Winchester
BLUE RIDGE
WASHINGTON
Annapolis
POTOMAC
Fredericksburg
Chancellorsville
VIRGINIA
RICHMOND
Yorktown
Fort Monroe
Petersburg
J. MANZ & CO., ENGR'S, CHICAGO.

VIRGINIA AND VICINITY.
GEN. LEE'S SECOND INVASION OF THE NORTH.

Outline of Events in the East, 1863.—Lee's second invasion of the North.

Prelude : Defeat of Union troops at Chancellorsville (May 2, 3 and 4, 1863).

Marches north into Maryland and Pennsylvania.

General Meade relieves General Hooker.

Confederate defeat at Gettysburg (July 1-3, 1863).

Confederates retreat to Virginia.

Results : Lee's second invasion a failure.

Both armies in the same relative position and strength as at the beginning of the year.

General Results for 1863.—General results much in favor of the North.

Mississippi river controlled by the North.

Chattanooga, the gateway to Georgia, held by Union troops, and the South becoming exhausted while the North is in the zenith of its power ; all these point to the final result. Both Generals Grant and Sherman say that there should have been no more fighting after 1863.

CHAPTER VIII.

IN THE WEST, 1864.

Changes Made.—During the winter of 1863–1864 plans were laid for the work of the next year. In March General Grant was made Lieutenant-General, the highest rank then known to the U. S. Army. This placed him in command of all the armies of the United States, and he was also directed to give his personal supervision to the Army of the Potomac. General Meade still remained commander of that army, though under the direct orders of General Grant. General Sherman was placed in command of the "Military Division of the Mississippi," which included all of the Mississippi valley, this being the position previously held by General Grant. General J. B. McPherson was given command of the Army of the Tennessee, the position made vacant by the promotion of General Sherman. General Schofield was sent to East Tennessee to command the Army of the Ohio.

Condition of Affairs at the Beginning of the Year 1864.—The Mississippi was firmly held by the Federals; but most of the country west of the river was held by the Confederates as far north as the Arkansas river. The northern troops occupied Pensacola, Key West, St. Augustine, Fort Pulaski and Port Royal along the Gulf and Atlantic coast, and controlled the waters of the Albemarle and Pamlico sounds. But Mobile, Savannah, Charleston and Wilmington were still in the possession of the Confederates.

The two armies in Virginia faced each other along the Rapidan and Rappahannock rivers. The Union troops under General Sherman were at Chattanooga preparing to move against Dalton, Georgia, where General Joseph E. Johnston was stationed ready to meet the advance.

The South, by conscription, called nearly every man and boy capable of bearing arms into the field.

At the North, by the first of May nearly a million men were enrolled in its armies, with over 600,000 ready for duty.

All the operations of the Union forces during the remainder of the war were directed by the master mind of General Grant, who planned to have all the armies "pull together."

General Sherman was ordered to move against General Johnston in Georgia; General Banks, with the aid of Farragut's fleet, was to capture Mobile; General Butler, at Fortress Monroe, was to move up the James river and attack Richmond from that direction; General Sigel was to pass up the Shenandoah Valley; General Meade was to destroy General Lee's army, and to capture Richmond.

All these were finally successful, though at the beginning some were failures, or partially so.

Sherman's Task.—General Sherman had with him at Chattanooga a force of about 100,000 men. His "objective" was Atlanta, defended by the Confederate army under General Joseph E. Johnston. The country from Chattanooga to Atlanta is very rough and mountainous, with narrow roads; altogether a very uninviting country in which to move an army. The Confederate army numbered from 50,000 to 75,000 men. But the conditions of the country, and the fact that the Southern army fought on the defensive behind breastworks, made the advantages nearly equal.

A body of soldiers, whether regiment, brigade, division or corps, halting for the night, when in the presence of an enemy, or forming for battle, occupying ground with a good outlook to the front, stacks arms and goes to work gathering logs, fence rails, stones, anything that will stop a bullet. These are piled in front, and a ditch dug behind, throwing the dirt forward upon them. In a short time a parapet that would stop even a cannon ball would thus be built. The Confederates being on the defensive, would thus protect themselves, while the Northern troops, being on the offensive, must either drive them from their intrenchments or go around—" flank " —them. For this reason, during 1864 both Generals Grant and Sherman were obliged to flank the enemy again and again to accomplish their object.

General Sherman had none too many men for the accomplishment of the work he set out to do.

The greatest problem of the campaign was one of supplies.

The Army of the Potomac was never very far away from tide-water, and as the North had full control of these navigable waters, it took comparatively few men to guard its line of supplies; and, as a rule, this army was abundantly supplied with all the equipments of war.

The gunboats and the transports on the Mississippi River had also made the problem of supplying the Army of the Tennessee, as it cut its way to the Gulf, a simple one.

But Sherman had a fighting force of 100,000 men, to be supplied by one single-track railroad running through a hostile country. Nashville was the principal depot of supplies. Its connection with the North is both by the Cumberland River and by the Louisville and Nashville Railroad. Chattanooga, the starting point of the campaign, is one hundred and thirty miles from Nashville. All the bridges, trestles, and culverts of the railroad, even as far north as Louisville, must be guarded from the enemies' cavalry and from a hostile population. But this was not all. Atlanta, the "objective" of the campaign, is over one hundred miles still further south; and this also must be guarded as the army moves southward.

The railroads in this long line of supplies were so poor and were broken so often by the enemy, that with all the energy of Sherman and his engineers, the Atlanta Army was scantily supplied.

The abundance of blackberries growing in the fields and along the roadside, and which were ripening at this time, saved the army from the scourge of scurvy.

The Atlanta Campaign.—May 6th, 1864, General Sherman started on his famous Atlanta campaign. It took him four long, bloody months to accomplish his task, with a loss of over 31,000 men. Dalton being protected on the north by mountains, General Sherman went south of it, striking the railroad at Resaca. Here a severe engagement occurred, in which the Confederates were defeated, and

General Johnston retreated south, and took a strong position at Allatoona Pass.

Sherman, knowing the strength of this position, did not attempt to take it, but passed around to the west.

This resulted in the severe battles of Dallas and New Hope Church, causing Johnston to give up Allatoona Pass. He made his next stand at Kennesaw mountain, just north of Marietta, and again Sherman, passing round to the west and south, compelled Johnston to leave this third very strong position, and fall behind the Chattahoochee river. It had taken two months of almost constant fighting to drive the Confederates from Dalton to the Chattahoochee river.

About this time the Confederate government, being displeased with Johnston's methods of defense, placed General J. B. Hood in command. When General Sherman crossed the Chattahoochee river, at Peach Tree creek General Hood attacked him with great force, but was driven back into Atlanta.

General Sherman, knowing that he could not entirely surround the city, passed a part of his army to the east of Atlanta, destroying the railroads there. But while at this work, again Hood came out to attack him, and was again defeated.

At this battle General J. B. McPherson, commander of the Army of the Tennessee, was killed.

This is known as the battle of Atlanta, though the city was not taken until several weeks later.

After destroying the railroads to the east, Sherman moved a part of his army to the west of the city. Here for the third time Hood came out to attack him, and was again driven back. This is known at the battle of Ezra Church.

Finally Sherman, leaving one corps at the Chattahoochee river to protect his railroad, moved the remainder of his army to Jonesboro, twenty miles south of Atlanta, where the Confederates were defeated, and General Hood, having all his railroad communications destroyed, gave up the city.

Atlanta was captured four months after the first move made from Chattanooga. General Sherman says: "Every foot of this should be sacred ground, because it was once moistened by patriotic blood; and over a hundred miles of it was fought a continuous battle of one hundred and twenty days, during which, day and night, were heard the continuous boom of cannon and the sharp crack of the rifle."

REVIEW OF THE ATLANTA CAMPAIGN.

OBJECT OF THE UNION ARMY.

If possible, to destroy the Confederate army, and obtain possession of Atlanta, the "Gateway of the South."

Battles: Rocky Face, Resaca, Dallas and New Hope Church, Kennesaw Mountain, Peach Tree Creek, Atlanta, Ezra Church, Jonesboro, with numerous smaller engagements, many of which might properly be called battles.

Result: Atlanta occupied by Union forces.

Losses: Union army in killed, wounded and prisoners, 31,000.

Confederates in killed, wounded and prisoners, 35,000.

Farragut at Mobile Bay.—In August, a little before the capture of Atlanta, Admiral Farragut gained possession of Mobile bay by passing the forts at its entrance, with his whole fleet.

The passing of these forts, like the passing of those at the mouth of the Mississippi river two years previous, was a very brilliant affair. Farragut had not only to brave the dangers of the forts, but must meet and defeat the Confederate ironclad navy just inside the bay; not only these, but a third obstruction lay in his way, and one which sailors most dread, in form of sunken torpedoes. While passing the forts one of these torpedoes accomplished its deadly mission in the destruction of a monitor. The forts surrendered a few days after the fight, thus giving the United States navy full command of Mobile bay, but the city of Mobile was not surrendered until the next spring, just before the close of the war. It was at this time

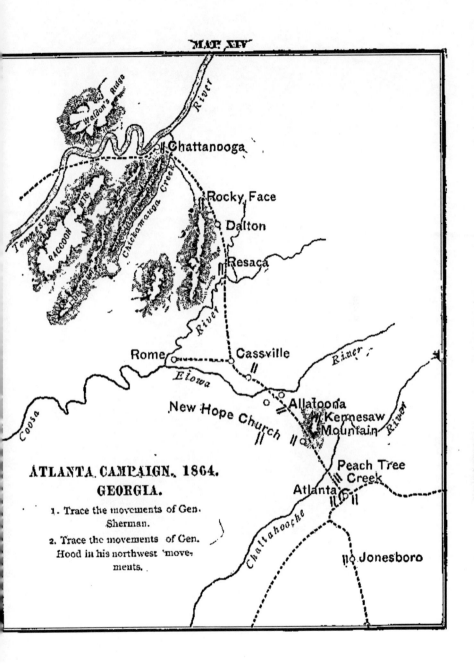

MAP XIV

Walden's Ridge

River

Chattanooga

Tennessee Mts.

RACOON MTS.

Chickamauga Creek

Rocky Face

Dalton

Resaca

River

Rome

Cassville

Eiowa

River

Coosa

New Hope Church

Allatoona

Kennesaw
Mountain

River

ATLANTA CAMPAIGN, 1864.
GEORGIA.

1. Trace the movements of Gen.
   Sherman.

2. Trace the movements of Gen.
   Hood in his northwest movements.

Peach Tree
Creek

Atlanta

Chattahooche

Jonesboro

Admiral Farragut became famous for having himself "lashed to the mast." The circumstances are these: wishing to see what was going on, he climbed into the rigging of the vessel in order to get above the mist and smoke that obstructed his view. Some of his officers, fearing that if wounded he might fall to the deck, tied him to the rigging. This circumstance has since become the subject of poetry and song.

It was the plan of General Grant to obtain possession of Mobile and open another line of supplies by way of the river and railroad through Montgomery to Atlanta. But, as we shall see, other events made this plan unnecessary.

General Hood's Movements North.—General Sherman's army at Atlanta drew its supplies from the North on a single line of railroad from Louisville, through Nashville and Chattanooga, to Atlanta.

It was necessary that every part of this line should be guarded, and it took what would make a large army to defend the line which supplied the army at the front.

General Hood, commanding the Confederate army, did not permit the Northern army to rest long at Atlanta. Taking advantage of General Sherman's long line of supply, he moved around to the north of Atlanta, hoping to so destroy the railroad as to compel the Union army to retreat to the north, and so lose what it had gained in the four months' fight.

The Confederates struck the railroad north of Kennesaw Mountain, destroying fifteen miles of it, as far north as Allatoona. In attempting to take this place, the Confederates were badly defeated.

While this battle was raging, General Sherman stood on Kennesaw Mountain, eighteen miles south, and by means of signal flags, sent over the heads of the enemy the famous message which has been perpetuated in the well-known song:

> " Ho! my comrades, see the signal
> Waving in the sky!
> Reinforcements now approaching,
> Victory is nigh."

CHORUS—"Hold the Fort, for I am coming," etc.

Moving around the strong position at Allatoona, Hood again de stroyed twenty miles of railroad around Resaca. General Shermar leaving one corps at Atlanta, rapidly followed the Confederate north with the remainder of the army, and drove General Hood fror the railroad. General Hood, moving to the northwest, occupie Florence and Corinth. By this move he threatened middle Tennes see, hoping thereby to draw General Sherman away from Georgia.

Sherman's March to the Sea.—General Hood's strategy had beer bold, rapid and brilliant, but unwise in the presence of such a mar as Sherman, who, instead of following Hood, returned and repaire his railroad. Hood moving north left all of Georgia open to th entrance of the Union army.

Seeing this open door, General Sherman sent General Thoma north with a part of his army to defend Tennessee, while with th other four corps and General Kilpatrick's cavalry, he started on hi famous " March to the Sea."

Before starting he destroyed all the railroad south of Dalton, and burned everything in Atlanta that could be of use to the enemy.

With but a small force in their front, with beautiful weather and a country full of all that was necessary to feed an army, th " March to the Sea " was something of the nature of a picnic to th soldiers.

The army, covering a belt of country from thirty to sixty mile wide, marched from Atlanta to Savannah, destroying railroads, cotton and public property, while in turn it feasted on the fat of the land As Savannah was held by the Confederate force, and was too strong a position to be taken at once, it was necessary to open communica tion with the Union fleet by way of the Ogeechee river, a few mile southwest of the city. This river was commanded by Fort McAllis ter, which was quickly captured, and soon a large number of vessels loaded with provisions, clothing and letters from home, steamed up the river.

After being cut off from communication with friends for weeks the letters were especially welcome. Savannah surrendered December 21, 1864, and General Sherman sent the following message to President Lincoln :

SAVANNAH, GA., December 22, 1864.

To his Excellency, President Lincoln, Washington, D. C.:

I beg to present you as a Christmas gift the city of Savannah, with one hundred and fifty heavy guns and plenty of ammunition ; also about twenty-five thousand bales of cotton.

W. T. SHERMAN,
Major General.

The message reached the President on Christmas eve, which caused great rejoicing throughout the North.

Franklin and Nashville.—General Hood, finding himself too far north to follow General Sherman into Georgia, moved north from Florence, Alabama, towards Nashville. Overtaking a part of the Union army at Franklin, the Confederates attacked it with great energy, but were repulsed with heavy loss.

General Thomas concentrated all his army at Nashville, except a sufficient force to hold the railroads leading to Chattanooga. About the middle of December, while General Sherman was closing in around Savannah, the other part of his Atlanta army, under General Thomas, was fighting a great battle, and winning a telling victory at Nashville, where the enemy was completely routed.

With but a remnant of his army, General Hood crossed the Tennessee river into Alabama.

The close of the year 1864 in the West found General Sherman in possession of Savannah, having completed his famous " March to the Sea," and General Thomas with a victorious army in complete possession of all Tennessee, with no enemy to oppose him.

MAP SHOWING THE RESULT IN THE WEST AT CLOSE OF 1864.

Shaded parts represent territory not yet occupied by the Union army.

Trace Sherman's march from Chattanooga to Savannah.

Hood started from Jonesboro, moving around to the west of Atlanta, striking the railroad at Allatoona and Dalton, then moved west through Decatur and Florence, crossing the Tennessee river, then north through Franklin to Nashville, where he was defeated.

Trace these movements.

The unshaded strip east of Vicksburg represents Sherman's incursion from Vicksburg in the early part of 1864.

All the railroads from Dalton to Savannah, represented in the unshaded parts, were destroyed by Sherman. Why?

Did Sherman occupy Augusta or Macon?

REVIEW OF THE WEST FOR 1864.

Atlanta Campaign.—
Rocky Face.
Resaca.
New Hope Church.
Kennesaw Mountain.
Peach Tree Creek.
Battle of Atlanta.
Ezra Church.
Siege of Atlanta.
Jonesboro.
Surrender of Atlanta (Sept. 2d).
Mobile Bay. Passing of forts by Farragut (Aug. 5th).
Hood's Northward Move.—
Hood's destruction of railroads.
Allatoona Pass.

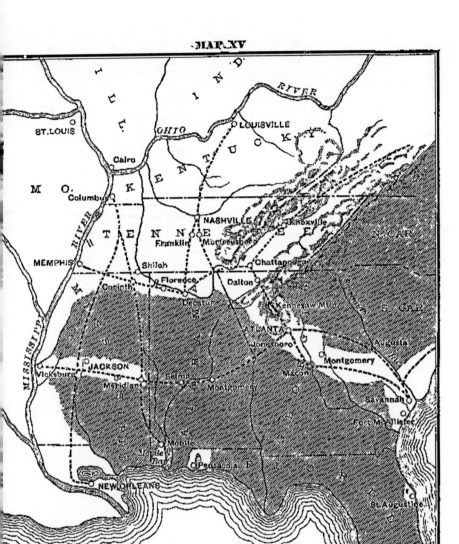

MAP XV

IN THE WEST.
SHERMAN'S MARCH THROUGH GEORGIA.
Shaded parts represent parts of the South not yet held by the
Union forces up to the close of the year 1864.

Hood invades Tennessee.
Battle of Franklin (Nov. 30th).
Battle of Nashville (Dec. 15th and 16th).
Resulting in destruction of Rebel army.
    Sherman's March to the Sea.—
Destruction of roads to Atlanta.
March through Georgia.
Fort McAllister captured (Dec. 13th).
Savannah captured (Dec. 21st).
Confederacy again cut in two.

CHAPTER IX.

WAR IN THE EAST, 1864.

General Grant, though commanding all the armies of the United States, took upon himself the immediate command of the forces in Virginia.

It is probable that history does not record more persistent, desperate fighting than was done from May 5th to June 5th, 1864.

The Union losses were in that time about 55,000 men. The Confederate losses are unknown, as no record has been preserved, but they are presumably not so great, as the Confederates were on the defensive and fought behind breastworks.

Battle of the Wilderness.—The Union army crossed the Rapidan river east of the position held by the Confederates. General Lee rapidly moving his army eastward struck the Union army while on the march south of the river. Here occurred the battle of the Wilderness, so called from the nature of the country in which it was fought. After two days trial of strength among the tangled woodland, neither party felt like again attacking the other.

Battle of Spottsylvania.—After resting one day at the Wilderness, General Grant moved his army towards Richmond, but was met at Spottsylvania Court-house by General Lee. Here for several days the bloody battle raged.

It was from this place that General Grant sent his world-famed message : " We have now ended the sixth day of very hard fighting. I am now sending back to Belle Plain all my wagons for a fresh supply of provisions and ammunition, and *purpose to fight it out on this line if it takes all summer."* General Grant going around to the east of the Confederates' position was in a position to again move towards Richmond.

The Bloody Angle.—It is well to take a closer view of some of the events of the war. The capture of the Bloody Angle at Spottsylvania will illustrate the desperate fury of some of the fighting. This is not an exception, but only an illustration of the multitudes of brave deeds by both the Blue and the Gray.

General Grant says: "Here a desperate hand-to-hand conflict took place. The men of the two sides were too close together to fire, but used their guns as clubs. The hand conflict was soon over. Hancock's corps captured some four thousand prisoners—among them a division and a brigade commander—twenty or more guns with their horses, caissons and ammunition, several thousand stand of arms, and many colors. Hancock, as soon as the hand-to-hand conflict was over, turned the guns of the enemy against him and advanced inside the rebel lines."

Also : " Lee massed heavily from his left flank on the broken point of his line. Five times during the day he assaulted furiously, but without dislodging our troops from their new position.

"His losses must have been fearful. Sometimes the belligerents would be separated by but a few feet. In one place a tree, eighteen inches in diameter, was cut entirely down by musket balls. All the trees between the lines were very much cut to pieces by artillery and musketry. It was three o'clock next morning before the fighting ceased. Some of our troops had been twenty hours under fire."

G. N. Galloway in the "Century," says : "Upon reaching the breastwork, the Confederates for a few moments had the advantage of us, and made good use of their rifles. Our men went down by the score ; all the artillery horses were down ; the gallant Upton was the only mounted officer in sight. Hat in hand he bravely cheered his men, and begged them to 'Hold this point.' All of his staff had been either killed, wounded or dismounted. At this moment, and while the open ground in rear of the Confederate works was choked with troops, a section of Battery C, 5th U. S. Artillery, under Lieutenant Richard Metcalf, was brought into action and increased the carnage by opening at short range with double charges of canister. This staggered the apparently exultant enemy. These guns, in the maze of the moment, were run up by hand close to the famous Angle, fired again and again, and were only abandoned when all the drivers and cannoneers had fallen. The battle was now to white heat. The rain continued to fall, and clouds of smoke hung over the scene. Like leeches we stuck to the work, determined by our fire to keep the enemy from rising up. Captain John D. Fish, of Upton's staff, who had until this time performed valuable service in conveying ammunition to the gunners, fell, pierced by a bullet. This brave officer seemed to court death as he rode back and forth between the caissons and cannoneers with stands of canister under his 'gum' coat. 'Give it to them, boys! I'll bring you the canister,' said he, and as he turned to cheer the gunners he fell from his horse, mortally wounded.

"Towards dusk preparations were made to relieve us. By this time we were nearly exhausted, and had fired three to four hundred rounds of ammunition per man. Our lips were encrusted with powder from 'biting cartridge.' Our shoulders and hands were coated with mud that had adhered to the butts of our rifles. When darkness came we dropped from exhaustion. About midnight, after twenty hours of constant fighting, Lee withdrew from the contest, leaving the Angle in our possession."

Soldiers Suffer as Well as Fight and Die.—The same writer, in speaking of the difficulties of the situation, says: "The storm which had set in early in the afternoon of the 11th of May continued with great severity, and but little rest was obtained during the night. Soon after dark, however, a remarkable change in the weather took place, and it became raw and disagreeable; the men gathered in small groups about half-drowned fires, with their tents stretched around their shoulders, while some had hastily pitched the canvas on the ground, and sought shelter beneath the rumpled and dripping folds. Others rolled themselves up, and lay close to the simmering logs, eager to catch a few moments sleep; many crouched about without any shelter whatever, presenting a pitiable sight."

Grant Again Moves.—General Grant, again moving by the "left flank," started for Richmond, and was again headed off by General

Lee at North Anna river. Finding the position at this place too strong, General Grant again moved around the Confederate army with the idea of getting between it and Richmond.

Cold Harbor.—This move brought on the battle of Cold Harbor, at which place the Union army met with a severe repulse.

General Grant Moves South of the James River.—After a few days around Cold Harbor, General Grant moved his whole army south of the James river, and attempted to take Petersburg, a position twenty miles south of Richmond. Failing in this, the siege of Petersburg and Richmond commenced. This siege continued until April 1st, 1865, a period of eight months. It will be remembered that while General Grant was moving overland, General Butler moved up the James river, occupying City Point and other strong positions. The fact of his being at this place aided very much in General Grant's movements south of the James river.

General Grant's movements from the Rapidan to Cold Harbor is called "The Overland Campaign," in contrast to the route taken by General McClellan two years before. While operating around Spottsylvania and North Anna, the army was supplied by way of Belle Plain or Fredericksburg and the Rappahannock river. While around Cold Harbor its supplies came by way of York river. After moving to the south of Richmond, the James river became the line of supply. It will be seen that General Grant made use of all the routes under discussion in the early part of the war.

EXERCISE ON MAP OF GENERAL GRANT'S OVERLAND CAMPAIGN.

Trace General Grant's line of operations.
What rivers did he cross?
Name them in order.
How many great battles were fought?

Operations in the Valley.—While General Grant was moving against the main Confederate army, General Sigel passing up the Shenandoah Valley was defeated at New Market. General Hunter superseding him in command, again moved up the valley, going as far as Lynchburg; but in retreating passed over to West Virginia and left unprotected that natural highway to the North, the Shenandoah Valley. General Early was quickly dispatched to Maryland defeating the Union troops at Monocacy, and came near capturing Washington before troops could be sent to its protection.

General P. H. Sheridan, who had commanded the cavalry of the Army of the Potomac during General Grant's movements, was now given command of the forces in the valley. He first defeated the Confederates at Winchester, then at Fisher's Hill, driving them from the valley. But it was too valuable for the Confederates to lose.

Again sending more forces into the valley, they attacked and at first defeated the Union army at Cedar Creek. This defeat occurred early in the morning, Sheridan being at Winchester, "twenty miles away." On hearing the firing, he rode rapidly to the front, meeting the fugitives from the defeated army. The enemy stopping to pillage the Union camps, Sheridan had time to stop and re-form his army. There was still time to win a victory, and on that afternoon the Union army moved against the Confederates, and before dark won a complete victory.

Never again did the South try to regain this famous valley.

MAP XVI

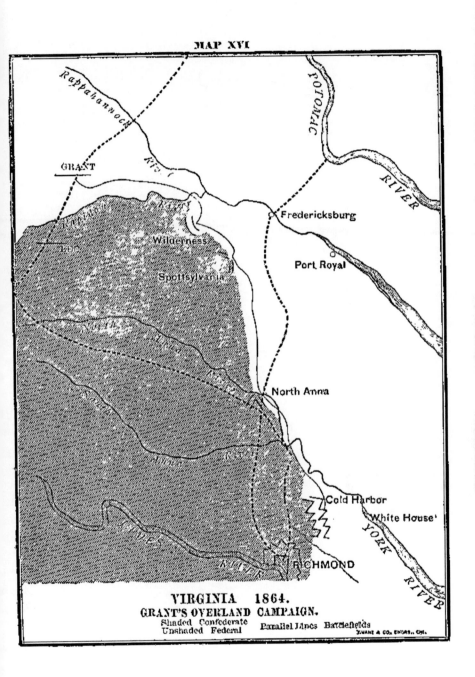

VIRGINIA 1864.
GRANT'S OVERLAND CAMPAIGN.
Shaded Confederate
Unshaded Federal
Parallel Lines Battlefields

REVIEW OF 1864 IN THE EAST.

Objective—Richmond.

1. General Butler moves up the James river and occupies City Point.

2. General Sigel moves up the Shenandoah Valley and is defeated at New Market.

3. General Hunter again moves up the valley and lets the door open for General Early to enter the North.

4. Battle of Monocacy. Washington in danger.

5. General Sheridan in command wins battles of Winchester (Sept. 19th), Fisher's Hill (Sept. 22nd) and Cedar Creek.

6. The valley cleared.

GRANT'S MOVEMENTS.

(a) Crosses the Rapidan river.

(b) Battle of the Wilderness (May 5–6th).

(c) Battle of Spottsylvania.

(d) Battle of North Anna.

(e) Battle of Cold Harbor.

7. Grant's whole army south of James river.

8. Siege of Petersburg.

9. Result: Union army gains a position which leads to the final defeat and surrender of Lee's army the next year.

General Results at the Close of 1864.—The fighting for this year had been more desperate and long continued than at any time previous.

At the close of 1864, in the West and South, General Thomas and General Sherman each had an army that could go anywhere in the Confederacy without serious resistance. General Thomas was in Tennessee preparing to move both east towards Virginia and south towards Selma and Montgomery. General Sherman at Savannah was preparing to move north through the Carolinas to cut another swath of destruction.

General Grant and General Lee were in a death grapple around Richmond and Petersburg. General Sheridan in the Shenandoah

Valley was ready to move south. Thus were Grant, Sherman, Thomas and Sheridan all converging toward Richmond, making General Lee's escape, with the only remaining Confederate army, almost impossible.

More than all the Confederates were exhausted. Men lost now could not be replaced. They had fought to the utmost of their strength and were fast losing ground.

EXERCISE ON MAP OF VIRGINIA AT CLOSE OF 1864, SHOWING RELATIVE POSITIONS OF THE TWO SIDES.

The shaded parts represent territory under Confederate control.

Note that General Grant's lines are south of Petersburg. His object was to get to the two railroads west of his lines.

Why?

He reached them in April of the next year.

In the meantime Sheridan had destroyed everything north of the James river.

Why, then, should Lee leave Richmond?

General Lee in retreating from Richmond withdrew his army from Petersburg and Richmond between the Appomattox and the James rivers. He then attempted to retreat to Burksville but General Grant from Petersburg headed him off.

Lee then attempted to reach Lynchburg, but General Sheridan got ahead of him at Appomattox Court-house, while General Meade was following. Lee then surrendered.

What direction did the armies move in the retreat?

MAP XVII

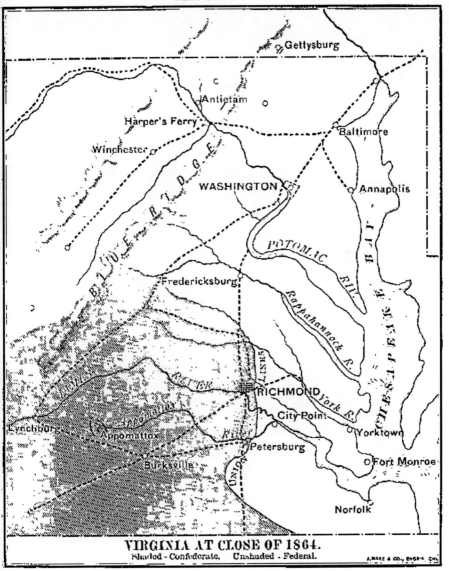

VIRGINIA AT CLOSE OF 1864.
Shaded - Confederate.   Unshaded - Federal.

J. MANZ & CO., ENGR'S, CHI.

CHAPTER X.

—

CLOSING EVENTS, 1865.

MOVEMENT OF WESTERN ARMIES.

Pontoons.—General Sherman moving from Chattanooga, through Atlanta, Savannah, Columbia and Fayetteville to Goldsboro, North Carolina, must cross at least twelve rivers. Of course all bridges, if any existed, were burned or otherwise destroyed by the enemy before the Northern army came near them.

While General Sherman is resting at Savannah, it may prove interesting to examine his plans for moving his army across these rivers.

A common pontoon bridge is made by anchoring boats side by side a few feet apart, and connecting them by timbers securely fastened. Across these timbers are placed board flooring. But General Sherman could not carry large boats. His pontoons were merely frames which could be fastened in shape of a scow-boat. Under and around these frames was stretched thick canvas cloth, this cloth forming the sides and bottom of the boat. Across these frail bridges all the immense trains, artillery and cavalry, as well as the infantry, passed.

Sherman Moves North.—In February, General Sherman having rested his army, loaded his wagons for another march, starting north through the Carolinas. At first his progress was much impeded through the swamps along the coast, but on reaching higher ground, with a small opposing force, he was soon in the heart of South Carolina.

Columbia was captured February 17th.

Much of the city was burned while in possession of the Northern army. The Union soldiers present made efforts to save the city, but in vain.

Destroying all railroads and public property on his route, General Sherman moved northeast through Fayetteville to Goldsboro, North Carolina. The Confederates, collecting what forces they could to resist the march of the Union army, placed them under General Johnston.

At Averysboro, and two days later at Bentonville, Johnston attempted to defeat a part of Sherman's army while on the march. Being frustrated in both of these attempts, he withdrew to Raleigh, and Sherman passed on to Goldsboro.

Here he met a Union force under General Schofield, and again the Union soldiers found food, clothing and mail awaiting them.

While General Sherman was going north, General Grant had sent a force against Fort Fisher at the mouth of the Cape Fear river. This fort, by the aid of the navy under Admiral Porter, was captured, and Wilmington soon after surrendered.

Charleston, South Carolina, was evacuated while Sherman was in the state. As a consequence of Sherman's movements, all of the Atlantic coast fell into the hands of the Union forces.

It will be remembered that General Schofield fought at the battles of Franklin and Nashville in December. How, then, do we find him in North Carolina in March? After the defeat of General Hood at Nashville, General Grant had ordered Schofield's army around by railroads and boats to North Carolina to aid Sherman in his march northward. So, again, much of the old Atlanta army was together in North Carolina. After allowing his army to rest at Goldsboro a few days, General Sherman was to have moved against Johnston at Raleigh, or against Richmond in aid of General Grant, but Sherman's army had fought its last battle, and earned its rest, which proved to be a long one.

While on the march to Raleigh the news of the surrender of General Lee reached Sherman's army amid the shouts and huzzas of the war-wearied veterans. A few days later Johnston surrendered to General Sherman, who, with his army, marched with light steps and lighter hearts to the grand review at Washington, then away to the far-away homes.

REVIEW—SHERMAN'S MARCH NORTH.

PLACES.

Columbia (February 17th).
Fayetteville (March 11th).
Goldsboro (March 21st).
Charleston surrendered (February 18th).
Wilmington surrendered (February 22d, 1865).

BATTLES.

Averysboro, Bentonville.

Wilson's Raid.—About the time that Sherman was completing his march northward, General J. H. Wilson started with a force of 12,000 cavalry from East Port, Alabama. Moving south he captured Selma and Montgomery, and was at Macon, Georgia, when the war closed.

While General Thomas was destroying Hood's army at Nashville, and General Sherman was eating out the heart of the Confederacy, and General Wilson with his cavalry was careering where he would, General Grant was holding the last Confederate army in his grasp at Petersburg and Richmond.

REVIEW OF THE ARMY OF THE POTOMAC.

COMMANDERS.

General Irvin McDowell.
General George B. McClellan.
General A. E. Burnside.
General Joseph Hooker.
General George G. Meade.

General U. S. Grant, also commander-in-chief of all the United States army.

In Shenandoah Valley, General P. H. Sheridan.

BATTLES FOUGHT.

Peninsular Campaign.—Bull Run, Yorktown, Williamsburg, Siege of Richmond, Seven Pines, Beaver Dam, Gaines' Mill, Savage's Station, White Oak Swamp, Malvern Hill.

Lee's First Invasion.—Second Bull Run, Harper's Ferry, South Mountain, Antietam, Fredericksburg and Chancellorsville.

Lee's Second Invasion.—Gettysburg.

Grant's Overland Campaign.—Wilderness, Spottsylvania, North Anna, Cold Harbor, Siege of Petersburg and Richmond, Five Forks, Sailors' Creek, Lee's surrender.

MAP OF SHERMAN'S MOVEMENTS FROM MAY 1, 1864, TO MAY 1, 1865.

The unshaded belt shows the territory covered by his army during that time.

Name the rivers in order which Sherman's army must cross in his two marches.   What two marches?

Name the large cities captured by him during the same time.

The light shade belt from Florence, through Selma, Montgomery, represents Wilson's raid in progress when the war closed.   Through what states did he march?

COMMANDERS OF THE CONFEDERATE ARMIES DURING THE CIVIL WAR.

ARMY OF NORTHERN VIRGINIA.

General P. G. T. Beauregard.

General Joseph E. Johnston.

General Robert E. Lee.

MAP XVIII

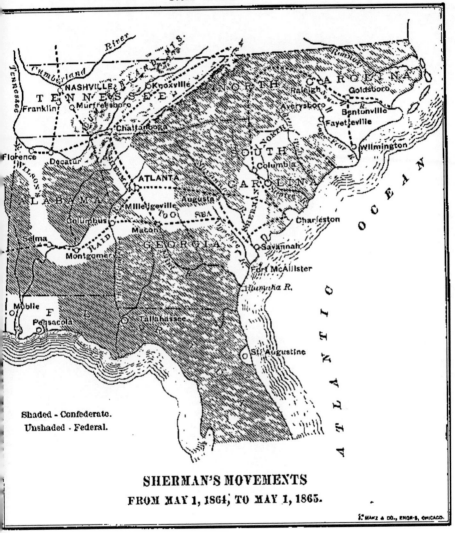

Shaded - Confederate.
Unshaded - Federal.

**SHERMAN'S MOVEMENTS
FROM MAY 1, 1864, TO MAY 1, 1865.**

MANZ & CO., ENGR-S, CHICAGO.

IN SHENANDOAH VALLEY.

General (Stonewall) T. J. Jackson.
General Jubal Early.

IN THE WEST—IN WESTERN TENNESSEE AND ALONG MISSISSIPPI RIVER.

General Albert Sidney Johnston (killed at Shiloh).
General P. G. T. Beauregard.
General Pemberton.

IN CENTRAL TENNESSEE AND GEORGIA.

General Braxton Bragg.
General Joseph E. Johnston.
General J. B. Hood.

CONFEDERATE ARMIES SURRENDERED TO THE UNION FORCES.

General S. B. Buckner to General U. S. Grant at Fort Donelson.
General Pemberton to General U. S. Grant at Vicksburg.
General R. E. Lee to General U. S. Grant at Appomattox Court House.
General J. E. Johnston to General W. T. Sherman in North Carolina.
General J. B. Hood's army destroyed in Central Tennessee by General George H. Thomas.
Other Confederate forces surrendered at close of war.

IN THE EAST, 1865—THE CLOSE.

During the winter General Grant had continued the siege of Petersburg, working his way around to the west with the intention of reaching the railroads that supplied Richmond. In March, while Sherman was moving north, General Sheridan with a large force of cavalry was moving south from the Shenandoah Valley. Passing down the James river near Lynchburg, he destroyed the canal along the James river, thereby cutting off the source of supplies to

Richmond. Moving around north of Richmond he reached General Grant at City Point.

During the latter part of March, General Grant moved General Sheridan with his cavalry to the west of Petersburg to attack the Confederates at Five Forks on the south side railroad. Here General Sheridan won a brilliant victory April 1st.

A BATTLE SCENE FROM FIVE FORKS.

[From Horace Porter in Century War Papers.]

"Sheridan now rushed into the midst of the broken lines, and cried out, 'Where is my battle flag?' As the sergeant who carried it rod up, Sheridan seized the crimson and white standard, waved it above his head, cheered on the men, and made great efforts to close up the ranks. Bullets were humming like a swarm of bees. One pierced the battle flag, another killed the sergeant who carried it, another wounded Captain McGonnigle in the side, others struck two or three of the staff officers' horses. All this time Sheridan was dashing from one point of the line to another, waving his flag, shaking his fists, encouraging, threatening, praying, swearing—the very incarnation of battle. It would be a sorry soldier who could help following such a leader.

"Ayers and his officers were equally exposing themselves in rallying the men, and these veterans soon rushed forward with a rousing cheer, and dashed over the earth-works sweeping everything before them, and killing or capturing every man in their immediate front whose legs had not saved him.

"Sheridan rode 'Rienzi,' the famous horse that had once carried him 'twenty miles from Winchester.' The General spurred him up to the angle, and with a bound, he carried his rider over the earth-works, and landed in the midst of a line of prisoners who had thrown down their arms and were crouching close under the breastworks.

"Some of them called out, 'Whar do you want us to go?' Then Sheridan's rage turned to humor, and he had a running talk with the 'Johnnies' as they filed past. 'Go right over there,' he cried, pointing to the rear, 'get right along now, drop your guns, you'll never need them any more. You'll all be safe over there. Are there any more of you? We want every one of you fellows.'

"Nearly 5,000 prisoners were captured at this battle. The cavalry commanded by the gallant Merritt had made a final dash, had gone over the earth-works with a hurrah, captured a battery of artillery, and scattered everything in front of them. Here Custer, Devin, Fitzhugh and the other cavalry leaders were in their element, and vied with each other in deeds of valor."

The next morning General Grant attacked the Confederate lines around Petersburg, driving them into the city, and taking many prisoners.

During this battle, while Jefferson Davis was attending church, he received a dispatch from General Lee saying that his lines were broken and that Petersburg and Richmond must be evacuated.

That night—April 3rd—General Lee withdrew from Petersburg and Richmond, hoping to reach Danville. But General Grant was too far south of him. Finding the Union army in his front, Lee attempted to reach Lynchburg to the west, but a large part of his trains and thousands of his men were captured.

Lee, finding General Sheridan in his front at Appomattox Courthouse, and General Meade following him, surrendered the remainder of his army to General Grant, April 9th.

Considering the long and bitter struggle, probably no terms of surrender known to history, were more magnanimous than those named by General Grant, of which the following is a copy:

GENERAL R. E. LEE,
    Commanding C. S. A.

GENERAL: In accordance with the substance of my letter to you of the 8th inst., I propose to receive the surrender of the army of N. Virginia on the following terms, to-wit: Rolls of all officers and men to be made in duplicate. One copy to be given to an officer designated by me, the other to be returned by such officer or officers as you may designate.

The officers to give their individual paroles not to take up arms against the Government of the United States until properly exchanged, and each company or regimental commander sign a like parole for the men of their commands. The arms, artillery and public property to be packed and stacked, and turned over to the officer appointed by me to receive them. This will not embrace the side arms of the officers, nor their private horses or baggage. This done, each officer and man will be allowed to return to their homes not to be disturbed by United States authority so long as they observe their paroles and the laws in force where they may reside.

Very respectfully,

U. S. GRANT,
Lieutenant-General.

These conditions were formally accepted by General Lee, and peace at last dawned upon the land.

" The charges were now withdrawn from her guns, the camp fires were left to smoulder in their ashes, the flags were tenderly furled— those historic banners, battle-stained, bullet-riddled, many of them but remnants of their former selves, with scarcely enough left of them on which to imprint the names of the battles they had seen— and the Army of the Union and the Army of Northern Virginia turned their backs upon each other for the first time in four long, bloody years."—PORTER.

A few days later, General Johnston in North Carolina surrendered his army to General Sherman on the same terms granted by General Grant.

In a few weeks all the other forces of the Confederacy, following the example of General Johnston, surrendered to the Union armies.

President Lincoln died on April 14th at the hands of the assassin, J. Wilkes Booth.

Mingled with the bells of rejoicing at the surrender of General Lee, were the tolling bells for the death of our beloved President.

Mingled with the sweets of peace were the bitter fruits of war. Probably not less than half a million graves of the divided American brotherhood, dotted the battle-fields of the sunny Southland.

The United States owed a debt of nearly three billion dollars at the close of the war. Over a million Union soldiers went back into the quiet pursuits of civil life without disturbance of any kind, probably the only occurrence of the kind known to history.

The South was not so fortunate on account of the overthrow of their peculiar social system. Much strife was continued there for many years. The slaves were not only made free, but by the XV amendment were also made voters.

The war and its lessons should not be forgotten. We should know the value of our inheritance. Other problems must be solved. Each generation has its own to solve. The generation of 1860 settled the question of *African* slavery and of a *permanent* Union. It is for the future generations to look well to other forms of slavery, and to .nake the Union worthy of permanency.